~FOREWORD ~

It's quick, quirky, and intensely personal. This book is a story of one woman's struggle with life in all its roughness and brutality. Through its pages, Julie Marlin chronicles how she became transformed from a rather mousy female who gave off the impression that she was afraid of her own shadow, to a victorious lioness who found the courage to take on no less than the devil. Through her very real and in many ways lonely battle, Julie charts a course for survival. It worked for her. It can work for others as well.

What happened to her could happen to any one of us. Illness, death, loss of dignity and control are all very human and very natural. What makes the author's experience unique is, first of all, the timing. Compressed into a segment of just two years she was compelled to face the sense of being displaced by moving to another state, the horrors of coping with breast cancer discovered at already an advanced stage, the tragic death of both of her parents killed unnecessarily, and the issues that come with parenting an only child whom (the journalist realized) she might not be able to live long enough to raise.

Many would crumble under the pressure of the circumstances which confronted this woman. Marlin, however, deciphered ways to meet each and every challenge. She began by employing the spiritual discipline of journaling. Interwoven among the accounts of her experiences as they were happening are memoirs of eclectic aspects of her past. As she plays the two off each other she becomes mysteriously able to put the present into perspective. Her analytical mind seems to be constantly racing unbeknownst to those around her who would appear to be in control. By describing the enemy, Marlin is able to render each (disease, death, and big business, health care and insurance agencies) all a little less threatening and a little less powerful.

The book includes much practical advice on how a person can learn to cope. It also offers a sense of catharsis for others facing troubles. Mostly it is pure heart. Readers will be brought to both tears and laughter. They can not miss the spunky spirit that practically leaps off every page. They will be inspired and come away feeling privileged that such a very intimate journal has been shared with others so graciously. I highly recommend LIVING ROOM to anyone who seeks to learn something of the stuff by which a real woman is made!

--Rev. Dr. Deborah Rahn Clemens

LIVING ROOM

A Visitor's Guide to Hell & Heaven

by Julie Marlin

Julie Marlin (signature)

Wild Grace • Red Hill, Pennsylvania

LIVING ROOM
A Visitor's Guide to Hell & Heaven
by Julie Marlin

Published by: WILD GRACE
                P.O. Box 194
                Red Hill, PA   18076   U.S.A.

Copyright © 2000 by Julie Marlin

Printed in the United States of America
10 9 8 7 6 5 4 3 2 1

Marlin, Julie
        Living Room: A Visitor's Guide to Hell & Heaven
First edition.

        Subject Headings include: Inspiration, Death & Grief,
        Autobiography, Breast Cancer

Foreword by Rev. Dr. Deborah Rahn Clemens
Some Illustrations by Rosalind Heitzman

ISBN 0-9700813-7-5

THANKS YOU'S ...

... to the many people who have provided their unique stories, and a willingness to take a part in this true story of one and a half years.

Thank you to the doctors and medical people: especially Pricilla Kistler, MD, Lewis M. Gill, M.D., to Sandra Corrado, MD, to Martin Hightower, MD, to the M.O.U. nurses, Lynn and Maureen, to the receptionist, Kathy.

The preparation of the manuscript has indebted me to others: The Hearthstone Town & Country, The Rev. Dr. Deborah Rahn Clemens, for review of the manuscript and for removing lots of the "ands," and to John Kevin, who made deep footprints for me to follow.

And especially I thank my friends and family, my husband, Tom, my daughter, Mariah, my brother Jack, and his wife Liz, and all those people that this story includes.

ACKNOWLEDGMENTS

All scripture quotations in this publication are from the Today's English Version — Second Edition © 1992 by American Bible Society. Used by Permission.

Love, Medicine & Miracles, Lessons Learned About Self-Healing from a Surgeon's Experience with Exceptional Patients by Bernie S. Siegel, M.D.©Copyright, 1986 by B.H. Siegel, S. Korman, and A. Schiff, Trustees of the Bernard S. Siegel, M.D., Children's Trust, Used by permission.

Air Bags & On-Off Switches — Information for an Informed Decision — Keeping the Benefits for the Many and Reducing the Risks for the Few, U.S. Department of Transportation, National Highway Traffic Safety Administration, DOT HS 808629 is a United States Government pamphlet.

ILLUSTRATIONS

The cover design, pen and ink drawings, and illuminations were created by the author with the following exceptions which were done by Rosalind Heitzman:

The Yawl in the Storm — with the poem, "Bon Voyage!"

The mountain scene on page 74
(with the title: "Your Footsteps Bring Joy To My Path — Peace to My Way")

Sketch of Colin on page 107

The angel mandela on page 108

The angel sketch at the top of page 109

Table of Contents

Perspective
The Journey Begins in the Waiting Room
You Can't Catch Me, I'm the Gingerbread Man
Thanksgiving and Ice
God Works in Mysterious Ways
The Telling
Reading Up

The Christmas Celebration
Dreams and an Opinion
Diagnosis
A Second Opinion
Living Room — Room for Living
The Seed Catalogue
Letters

Hair Today, Goon Tomorrow
A Will is a Plan the Planner Won't See
Second Treatment & Entirely Too Much Television
A Port in Any Storm
Half-Way
All Purpose Hopes & Fears to Hold Onto

Author's Preface

Have you ever gone down a dark path on a moonless night, groping for a footing, then thinking of the possibility of creatures lurking in the shadows, so in order to dispel the fear you have tried singing? It works. That solitary voice humming off key in the darkness sets things right. Singing must be like sonar for the angels. When you are singing the angels can find you in the dark and guide you safely through. Your lonely song seems to make everything peaceful. Some of us find that writing brings that same kind of peaceful relief from the darkness.

After singing, I have always considered a pen my second line of defense when danger threatens. I took a pen along for those life and death drills we had in elementary school: tornado practice when we huddled in the hallways covering our heads, and for those cold war air raid drills when we hid under our desks to avoid some imagined threat of nuclear annihilation. As a child, I was sure that if any real tragedy befell me I would be safe with a pen because I believed that God could read my handwriting even when no one else could.

Since God, and sometimes only God, can recognize the music in my song, and can read my writing and decipher my spelling I usually enter into both singing and writing prayerfully. Then, because God is God I find not only comfort but also inspiration.

But this book did not come to me as one of those serene little moments of music and inspiration. This story fell into my living room like a huge flaming meteor. While everything around me was crashing and burning, and I was grasping for a pen, suddenly, before me, rising up from the smoke and ashes was a computer-- with spell check.

When I started writing this, I thought it would be a book about cancer. A book about cancer, it seems, should offer some kind of useful information about cancer. But this is not a book about cancer. This a story about life as told in the context of cancer. I feel that I am alive to write this now because of God's grace and also because of advances in medical knowledge and the skills of doctors. The doctors are the heroes and I thank them. They are individually named in the "Thank You's." Even as I have been about the task of entering my handwritten journal into a computer's memory, the medical community has been learning new things, and changing. So too, have individual doctors changed their ways of thinking. As surely as my own thoughts become outdated as soon as I have new thoughts, so also would the medical know-how of doctors become out of date quickly. I have thus chosen to fictionalize doctors, rather than to time-freeze these real people. So, in this, otherwise true story, I have changed the names of the real doctors and medical people and I have also created a completely fictional doctor, "Dr. Apple," who represents a collection of my real conversations and experiences with various doctors.

While I am listing disclaimers it should be noted that some of these theological wanderings have strayed from the path that has been trodden and shaped by traditional Christian doctrine. I was well aware of this, so I called a friend whom I know to have a wide, clear perspective of the history and tradition of Christian thought and she read this manuscript. She cautions especially against a kind of dualism which separates the physical and spiritual and threatens some of the essential aspects of Christian doctrine. I pass her caution on to you, the readers. Having this thing called human nature marking my ways I do tend to separate things into twos while I am learning and thinking about them. This trait is not always helpful. The frog, for example, does not live after it is dissected even though the student doctor has just learned how to save its life. Perhaps one day I will outgrow this method of learning, but, for now, reader be warned.

Bon Voyage! Sail forth in joy
Upon life's great adventure
In your fragile craft
So small, and unaccustomed to the sea.

There shall be days of sailing smooth
Which are for thankfulness
For one another, and for love;

And hours when you're becalmed,
When time and waters both stand still.
These are for patience, and bring solitudes
For plummeting love's depths.

But when the winter storms
Lash fury through the night
To beat your boat,
And nearly sink your dreams,
Cling tightly then to one another --
'Tis strengthening the bond --

And fear not,
For that Power which tugs your sails,
Ripping them and tossing you asunder,
Is the same Power that loves you most,
And promised safe harbor in the dawn.

Rosalind

CHAPTER 1

Perspective

ere we are at the shifting of the millennium, and we have some awesome phenomena waiting in the wings to become our Armageddon. Will it be earthquake, wind or fire? Maybe the weather is a character in the drama. Will it be aids, nuclear error, or biological warfare? Will it be cancer?

Cancer is a great plague for our time. It has all the useful features of the judgment that befalls humankind when people imagine that the powers of good and evil battle. It chooses a large percentage of the population, seemingly at random, so it must reflect some force beyond our human understanding. No one knows why one person gets cancer, and another does not. The scientists are the most baffled of all, it seems. The myriad of theories cover every possible sin and activity known to Twentieth Century human beings: pollution, stress, smoking, drugs, alcohol, eating fast food, cooking with electricity, irradiated foods, sitting too close to the cathode ray tube. Or perhaps cancer comes from food additives or mold, or too much fat, or crash dieting, antiperspirants, allergies or bruises, or maybe playing the guitar does it. Maybe the cause is electro-magnetic fields around power wires, or radon in the soil, or asbestos in the walls. Maybe it is from having too few children too late in life, or maybe just estrogen, or genetics, or it's just a part of aging. If it all seems just too confusing, then blame the immune system. It could be a virus, or rats— no wait, rats were the Fourteenth Century plague. Nowadays the rats are incorporated into the big salvation plan -- science.

Since these scientific searches lack the definitive answer, then it must be a religious problem. But religion was relegated to cover only "things unseen" back in the age of "Enlightenment." And cancer is visible. Oh, but the cause is yet unseen. So let us say that cancer comes to the "bad" people, who are so irresponsible that they don't notice the seven deadly danger signals: lumps, moles, splotches, bleeding, or another triad of miscellaneous changes. That is how we come to live out our whole lives fearing lumps and changes. Well, some of us fear. I always have feared. I still do.

So, I have been day-tripping to Hell and back for little visits with the powers of darkness. Fear takes us on these strange journeys. Courage keeps us "just visiting". Courage gives us a way out. And so, I share my journey with you as a visitor's guide for travelers like me, who wish to come back from Hell and travel again another day perhaps to a more beautiful spiritual get-away like... say, Heaven for example.

Oct. 96

The Journey Begins in the Waiting Room

Journeys to Hell often begin in waiting rooms. Waiting rooms for lawyers, doctors, photographers, the college dean, the boss, whomever, they are all the same. They are holding tanks for stress, equipped with stiff chairs that look nice together, magazines, and air conditioning. They are monitored by receptionists, who can answer the phone for less money than the person whose phone it is. Although my journey just seems to begin in a waiting room, it actually began in my imagination.

I imagined I was dying of cancer, because I found a lump in my breast. I imagined my husband would want no part of this kind of affliction what with having to deal with the pain, the loss, and the tremendous expense of it all, all at once. I imagined he would leave. My daughter would be left alone on a sort of ethereal shore, as I was sinking in the darkness of a vast unknown sea of death. I started writing her a letter which soon became this journal. I spent my waiting room time reading pamphlets, and writing in this journal.

Since a waiting room was a definite improvement over my imagination, in September, 1996, I made an appointment with Dr. Williams. This was where I committed the "original sin" of cancer. I let the appointment setter believe that I always had a lump in my breast, so there was no hurry to deal with it. She said it probably needs to be checked anyway. In cancer hell the rules are simple. Good people act immediately. Bad people wait.

When we moved to this Pennsylvania community recently I was glad to find the small town feature of a family doctor. As a very young child we visited the family doctor in our small town in Illinois by walking to a large brick house on the corner. The doctor, who seemed to be a friend of my parents, had a family in town. That is why, I thought, they called him a "family" doctor. Perhaps the real reason he was a "family" doctor was because his father was a doctor, and his father's father was a doctor.

Dr. Williams was in every possible definition, a "family" doctor. In this small Pennsylvania town, Dr. Williams lived in the brick house on the corner, where she also had her office. She was a third generation family doctor. Her father, "Old Doctor Williams" lived with her, as did her small children.

She is well known as a thorough and caring doctor, so the wait to see her was a very long one. First there was a wait to get an appointment since we were new to the community. Then once the October appointment date arrived the wait inside the waiting room began. I waited while others with real infirmities, not just fears and imaginings, were taking their turns to be seen by Dr. Williams. When finally my turn came Dr. Williams took just a minute to assess that I would need to move on to two more waiting rooms: first to the "Women's Health Clinic," for a mammogram, then to a surgeon for a lumpectomy. She took a half hour to listen, and she knew that I would really need a surgeon who had the ability to talk and listen, because I was very fearful, and I deal with fear by balancing imagination and actually understanding, learning all I can about the problem, until at last, I learn that reality is less atrocious than my imagination.

While I was waiting for these opportunities to wait in some more waiting rooms I could feel the lump growing bigger, and hotter every day — like a monster child growing inside my breast to absorb the space left by my beautiful human child outgrowing her need for me.

Nov. 96
In November my turn for a mammogram came.

The technician at the Women's Health Clinic had a name, but I didn't read her name tag-- so I will just call her "Madam X-Ray" for the purposes of this dialogue which I had recorded that day in my journal.

MADAM X-RAY: *(As she read over my life history fit into "PLEASE PRINT/USE INK" blank spaces)* So, you

think you have found a lump in your right breast—
it says— you had a cyst in that breast 18 years ago.
Was it aspirated?

ME: No. It just went away.

MADAM X-RAY: Then how do you know you had a cyst?

ME: Well, it was there, then it wasn't. The doctor then
       called it "probably a cyst."

MADAM X-RAY: *(Marking a question mark on my chart.)*
       So, you don't know that you had a lump there. But
       now you think you have one. Do you think you can
       locate this lump you thought you found, again?

ME: *(Separating the panels of the gown to show her the
       lump standing right up on the surface of my otherwise
       small breast. It was perfectly visible to the naked eye.
       I tried very hard not to see it, and yet I saw it. I
       answered.)* Yes, it is easy to see.

MADAM X-RAY: Well if you think you can find it again, try
       and place this sticker in the general area.

*(She handed me a tiny dot sticker, and I stuck it dead center on
the lump.)*

ME: Okay, done.

*(Then the smashing and tugging project began. I was not at
all surprised that it hurt, since I had mammograms fairly
regularly after that cyst scare 18 years ago. I know it hurts
to have a mammogram and I know the technicians always say
"This is just pressure. It doesn't hurt." I think part of their*

*training must include practicing the line "This doesn't hurt."
in a flat, lifeless tone, amid screaming and wailing. It's a
technique that was perfected by school nurses in the '50's who
gave polio shots to gymnasiums full of screaming children.
"Now this won't hurt". Madam X-Ray had it down perfectly.)*

MADAM X-RAY: That doesn't hurt.

ME: My breasts are always sore this time of the month.

MADAM X-RAY: What does the time of month have to do
    with it?

ME: *(Trying hard to believe she really didn't know.)* PMS
    makes my breasts sore. Don't other women say that
    too? *(Could I really be the only woman in the world
    who had this experience?).*

MADAM X-RAY: PMS?

ME: Pre Menstrual.... *(I suddenly realized my gray hair put
    me in the non-PMS group in her mind. Does she really
    not know that gray hair is optional these days? Or
    perhaps she came from the land of the ferns and really
    had no idea that there ever was such a thing as PMS.)*

MADAM X-RAY: This may pinch a little.

ME: Yikes!

MADAM X-RAY: Some women don't complain at all.

ME: How many more squashes do you need?

MADAM X-RAY: Just one for now, then I will get them developed, and see if we can go on to the other side.

ME: I have PMS on that side too.

MADAM X-RAY: Sure, you do. Now, this doesn't hurt. It is just pressure.

(She sent me into the dressing room to wait, since the waiting room seems to have a dress code, and I was only wearing a gown. It was nice to have a moment away from Madam X-Ray and her giant machine. Through the thin door I could hear another technician, and another woman in the room. I could hear their conversation, and I was assured that I was not the only woman who had confused "a little pressure" with something that actually hurt.)

This whole project is a lot like being the magician's assistant that gets sawed in half. There is a big piece of expensive equipment at the center, and lots of doors, and panels, a places to go wait, and there is one magic person who knows what is actually happening. Everyone else just guesses by the reaction of the magician. Oh yes, and there is one other big similarity. The grand finale is that you get sliced and diced, or possibly, you disappear, who knows?

("Madam X-Ray" returned from developing my "films," and my turn resumed. But things were much different now. She had seen my pictures.)

MADAM X-RAY: You can come back in now honey. Are you alright now?

ME: Yes... Well, you know better than I. What did the x-rays show?

MADAM X-RAY: Technically, they were excellent — Oh, don't worry honey, we don't have to hurt you there any more. I am so sorry. We just have to do three exposures of the left breast. *(She gently adjusted the plates of glass on the machine.)* Is that comfortable?

ME: Well I still have PMS...

MADAM X-RAY: Oh, I am so sorry. I will be as gentle as I possibly can.

ME: So, what did the x-rays show?

MADAM X-RAY: Oh, we can't tell you that. The technician has to assess them, and your doctor will talk with you. Are you alright? We are all done now.

So I learned two new things about cancer that day: One is that I have it, and no one wants to tell me that. So no one did. The other is that cancer changes the personalities of everyone who comes near a person who has it. People who know the unspoken answers, like technicians and doctors, and other miscellaneous chart-readers are sucrose. Most everyone else just wants to guess how long you have to live. And those are two good reasons not to tell.

"You Can't Catch Me, I'm the Gingerbread Man"[1]

Dr. Finn's waiting room was nice--not too cold, not too hot--plants— lots of magazines--music--windows--art--a fish tank— Dr. Finn has fish? His waiting room even has puns. It is a place designed for prayers, and farewells.

I rehearsed my childhood fears. I remembered why I dreaded medical experiences.

Sugar and spice all flattened with a rolling pin makes that infamous gingerbread man who popped off the tray, and ran away shouting, "Run, run as fast as you can, you can't catch me, I'm the Gingerbread man." As flat and manufactured as he was he still got up and ran... ran.. so he wouldn't get eaten.

Then there were those gingerbread children encircling the witches house who were eventually rescued by Hansel and Gretel. That is the gingerbread story I wanted to impart to the surgeon before he stuck me with a needle.

[1]*Hansel and Gretel*, and *The Gingerbread Man* are traditional children's stories.

My mother, and "the woodcutter," (played in my life by my dad) pondered the young family's financial woes. In my heart, I knew if they did not have children, they would be rich. So I was not surprised one day, when I was obviously coming down with something and was to be even more of an expense, that my dad (in the role of the woodcutter) didn't go to the usual family doctor. Instead we went "deep into the forest" or was it the city, and there we waited, not in a room at the doctor's house, as I had been accustomed, but in an *Office Waiting Room!*

My dad stayed in the waiting room while I was escorted into a stainless steel chamber with a strange clean man in a white coat. There was no conversation, just a lot of activity -- preparation for something, like cooking. I could see it all clearly now. This was the witch's gingerbread house. Only, here, the children were flattened and cooked into this cold steel--stainless steel--stainless steel tables, stainless steel chairs stainless steel cupboards. I could feel the warmth leaving my body. My fingers were icy cold.

I don't remember the rescue at all, but somehow I got back home, and no one, again, spoke of the day that I was supposed to have been made into a stainless steel table. But it stuck in the archives of my imagination, with the monsters under the bed.

The next time I had an appointment to see the doctor I took the heroic stand of the gingerbread man. I ran, ran as fast as I could, and sure enough, my mother and the nurse and even the doctor, still wearing his white coat, all ran through the waiting room, out the door, and down the street after me. But unlike the gingerbread man, they caught me, and took me back into the chamber of stainless steel children. Well, since I had run away everyone had to stand guard. That meant the nurse and my mother were in the room with me, and the doctor could not perform his incantations, so my day as a table would have to wait, again.

On the way home I learned that I was a very big embarrassment to my mother. I knew the next medical event would have to be on the doctor's terms. So I prepared for that day by assessing my life. I prayed that if it was possible I may be spared, but if not, then, that God make me an angel with Grandma Munro.

The next visit to a doctor's office was peaceful, as I knew it must be. I promised I wouldn't run, or "make a scene." So at the first glimpse of that cold silver steel I passed out. That somehow worked. I did not become any kind of medical apparatus, and nothing happened to me. From that day on, until very recently, at every threat of stainless steel administered by white coats, no matter if it is a table, sink or needle, I simply prepare to die, my blood vessels shut down, I hold my breath, and drop to the floor...I could "die" before they could take me. Death on my own terms was, and still is, better than life as a stainless steel table.

As the years went on I had to be anaesthetized for everything — blood tests, dental work, whatever. And if the anaesthetic was supposed to be breathed, as in the dentist's office, or when preparing for surgery, I held by breath until I passed out, then I could wake up on my own terms.

I was a totally dreadful patient. On that day in Dr. Finn's waiting room I wrote in my journal "I still am a Doctor's worst nightmare. So when other people may be at the 'why me?' stage of grief[2] over their illness, with me, it is the doctor who is saying 'Why him?'"

Dr. Finn not only has the best waiting room, he also has all the best doctor features: He is tall, clean, wears a white coat, just like the play doctors on drug ads on T.V. But the thing I like best about him was that he talked to me, and he spoke honestly.

My first appointment in his office was the first Tuesday in December. He had already seen the great quality mammograms taken in November, so he already knew more about me than I was supposed to ever know, and despite his honest nature, he chose to keep a secret. He looked at the lump. He also listened to my real heart — my fears and my hopes. So I didn't pass out when the stainless steel wand waved over my breast.

The painful part of the aspiration was seeing the grim faces of the nurse and the doctor. Something was deposited in a small vile of green liquid on the counter. The test was done except for the great "unknown" test results. It was time to talk about the great "unknown" 4 cm. lump.

My husband was invited into the examining room, and Dr. Finn explained surgery would be needed to biopsy the lump.

I expected Dr. Finn to say, only 1 in 10 lumps is malignant. I knew that statistic. It was my favorite thing to hear. I wanted Dr. Finn to say that, but he didn't. I looked at

---

[2]The stages of grief are explored and defined in *On Death and Dying*, by Elisabeth Kubler-Ross, Macmillan,© 1969.

the green vile, and he saw me glance, then stepped in front of the counter where it was so I couldn't see it. What would I see if I could? This was a lab/microscope thing, too tiny to see with the naked eye, so why was it necessary to hide it?

He asked me the battery of questions I would soon have committed to memory. Do you smoke? Drink? Etc. etc. Have you ever had a severe injury to your breast. I answered, "Well I just had a mammogram." Dr. Finn said that doesn't count.

I still wanted Dr. Finn to say "Only one in 10 lumps is malignant." But as much as I wanted to hear it, he didn't say that. He said if it is malignant, an oncologist will talk with me after the surgery, and then I would need radiation or chemotherapy. But he still didn't say, "only one in 10 is..." So I asked, "What are the statistics?" He said, "you don't want statistics right now. One in three people gets cancer in their lifetime. There, that is a statistic." Okay, I was satisfied. Obviously, he was not thinking at all of nine benign lumps. "So how much of my breast will you cut off for the biopsy?"

Thanksgiving and Ice

Thanksgiving was square in the middle of this, like a buoy marking the channel for a ship named "life goes on". My parents came over for the day from New York. Since we moved to Pennsylvania we were only four or five hours apart. For my dad who seemed to thrive on opportunities to cross New York City, and drive into the Pennsylvania mountains, that meant they could come over for dinner whenever we wanted to get together. We had celebrated Dad's birthday at our dining room table in October, and now it was time to share another celebration dinner. The weather forecast called for a little rain that day. But when the rain started, it was barely 30 degrees, and we were all concerned that the drive home might be icy and treacherous for them. We begged them to stay over, and drive back after the roads could be properly salted. But Dad was meeting with a family the next morning at his Long Island church, and he did not feel he could change that meeting. Also, I think the opportunity for adventure was calling him.

He always chose adventure, when it was being served. Just four years earlier, when we were all living in Ohio, Dad was a pastor of a rural church. A major source of gratification for him was his youth work. He kept up with the local youth culture, so it was not surprising to find him listening to a local Rock n' Roll station. When this station offered a contest, he entered it. Maybe no one else did, or maybe he was just lucky. But he won. The prize was a chance to jump from an airplane with a parachute while the adventure was being covered by the radio broadcast. On the day scheduled for him to collect his prize, Mariah and I went to the small airport in the middle of a cornfield that winter morning at 5:30. We met Mom and Dad there, along with a parachute team, and the people from the radio station. All of the jumpers suited up. Dad was given a leather helmet that looked like a cartoon of a WWII fighting Ace. The disc jockey wore a white jump suit with spangles, reminiscent of Elvis.

As the radio personality tried to keep the banter going in the airport building, while the plane was being prepared, he put his microphone to Mariah, the only young teen present. I think he assumed she was his fan. "So what brings you out here this morning? Did you come to see your old buddy "Steve the Voice that Rocks" jump from an airplane?" Mariah answered, "Rev. Heitzman is my grandfather. I came to see him jump." "What! The Rev. is a grandfather! Well, what other secrets do you have for us?" He cut to a commercial.

"How old is this guy anyway?" My mother who had just been terrified by signing the release forms was in tears. "He is too old for this. I don't know why he is doing it! He is 75 years old. When will he grow up?"

Now for my mother, who would have bought seatbelts for our sofas if they were available, Dad's off-beat sense of adventure was the most catastrophic dimension of their whole fifty plus years together. While she never in her life had so much as dinged a car door, Dad paid speeding tickets like they were his light bills. He learned to drive at twelve in a cornfield, when Ford models were called by alphabet letters, not zodiac signs. And he had been driving pretty much the style of a Keystone Cop ever since. For Dad, jumping from an airplane on a frosty winter's morning was the crem d'la crem of great adventures. It had speed, beauty and media coverage as well.

 The radio broadcast was mainly the disc jockey screaming, "How does the Rev. stay so calm?" They all landed safely, the disc jockey, the professional parachute instructors, and my dad. I took lots of pictures, I think the enlargements I had made of him were his all time favorite Christmas gift.

So, here we were at Thanksgiving dinner, thanking God for our blessings. I was thankful for these people. And I also offered a silent prayer for my medical thing of which I was secretly in the midst. I chose not to mention it at that time. I wanted to talk about it in a time and setting that I picked, not just the day that was the fourth Thursday in November.

Now the ice was coating the road. From the dining room we could look out the big bay window, where the view of rural Pennsylvania is framed by roadways. We could see that the few cars which had ventured out were barely creeping along. Even before we had finished dessert Dad stood up and announced that they were leaving before the weather got "bad." And ten minutes later they were on the road. We turned on TV to find all the channels covering the breaking news story. The weather had completely paralyzed the East Coast. The reporter said he had just come from New York to Philadelphia, and they counted as many a twenty accidents in a single mile. We stayed focused on the news. Then, just four and half hours later, the phone rang. Dad's familiar cheerful voice said, "Just wanted you to know we got home fine." I was amazed. "The news said the roads were virtually impassable!" Dad said, "The wrecks were in the other lanes."

Dec. 96

God Works in Mysterious Ways

The Pre-op tests were the dreaded Part I of my hospital experiences. While I nervously waited in the plush waiting room, guise to rooms of stainless steel tables and needles, "Susan", a woman I had met recently, kept flitting up and down the hallways of the hospital in and out of the waiting room. She seems familiar with the hospital. Maybe she is here for some treatment, I surmised, though she apparently isn't sick.

My turn came and I was escorted to the great hall of needles, a large room with chairs and gurneys and few pieces of cloth hanging from wire clothes lines symbolizing modesty between various configurations of steel cabinets and sinks. It was a virtual forest of tubes and syringas. I was strapped into a 1950's style fiberglass chair. A head nurse came over with my charts. She had an other-worldly air of authority, but her hands were all bandaged! She held out her bandaged appendages to show me, and said "Our temp will draw the blood." I could hardly believe I was living through this. A temp? A temp? I work as a temp in offices, and I happen to know, temps absolutely do not know what they are doing. I felt the tug of the seat belt, and I knew I must be trying to run.

"Where's the temp!" Shouted the great white nurse. In came Susan! "Oh dear God, it's Susan!" I must have said that aloud because she recognized my distress. Then I realized, Susan could never be the stainless steel witch. She's a human being like me. She hugs people. She could see my fear, and she hugged me. Then she said, "let's pray together." She held me in her arms, and prayed "Jesus be with us. Jesus be with Mrs. Marlin." She was the first, and only nurse, doctor, or temp who has ever found my vein on the first try. I didn't pass-out. "Thank you Jesus!" And thank you Susan.

December 11

The lump biopsy was scheduled as "outpatient surgery." All the paperwork I could sneak peeks at called it a partial mastectomy. I asked about what that meant. I was told they would not take my lymph nodes and all the breast tissue. When they take everything it is a radical mastectomy. The most up-to-date protocols were saying taking the lump and surrounding tissue, along with radiation treatment was better than a radical mastectomy with no follow-up radiation. The plan was, if it is malignant they would take the lymph nodes too, and test them, then use chemotherapy and radiation to attack hidden cancer cells.

"Does that mean this surgery may include my lymph nodes?" I asked.

The doctor answered, "No, that would be done later if needed. That is why this is outpatient surgery."

The ultimate waiting room was the waiting place for surgery. This is a wide place in the hospital hallway where the air conditioner blows drafts over the utilitarian green walls, where racks of supplies are stored, and nurses sign-up for days off and make their personal calls. Ceiling grates, and flickering fluorescent tubes replace any possibility of windows. It is in this storage room where one must wait all alone. That is the place for those "Prepare to live or die" choices, and to pray the "but not my will, but thine" prayers and you wonder if the devil is trying to prove human frailty to God. I was prepared for the drug needles, and prepared for the slicing and dicing. I was prepared for death. I was not prepared for the complete ugliness of the situation. A little flower painted on the ceiling, or even one of those obnoxious yellow smiley faces would have taken me on a completely different tour. But Hell has it's protocol. A strange looking little man in a doctor costume kept flitting in and out.

The phone rang and rang. A nurse finally came in and answered it. She pushed some buttons on the switchboard to page another nurse, who came in and took the call. She began to cry. The first nurse comforted her. It seems her child had been in a playground accident at school, and had a head injury. He was being rushed to this hospital, now.

On medical shows on television the usual plot is that doctors and nurses face horrors of their own, and the patients are usually set pieces. I thought that was just on television.

Now the nurse with the injured son came over to me, and prepared needles and tubes and hung up a bag of clear liquid over my gurney. The other nurse asked if she was alright. She said she would finish up what she had to do, to "take her mind off of it." I suggested there was already enough stainless steel in the room. She had no idea what I was talking about. I told her my name, and that it was my right breast and that I wasn't supposed to get the kind of anesthetic that puts you out. I wanted to cover all the bases, and if possible help her keep her mind on her work. She said she wasn't going to give me any drugs now. She was just starting the IV. That sounded like a good plan to me, but somehow it still involved a needle, a tube, and a plastic bag of something fluid hanging over me.

She left, and a few minutes later that strange looking little man in the doctor costume returned, and announced to me that he was the anaesthesiologist. He read a list of bad things that could happen to me. I actually found that comforting, since I had a file of bad things in my imagination that included all that stuff and more. I was going to pull it out and review it if they had pretended that nothing bad could happen. I always want to be prepared by thinking the worst. And just as he predicted, I would forget this. At least I forgot the blow by blow details of what he said.

I do remember being wheeled into the operating room, under a different ceiling grate. Dr. Finn came in. I reminded him of my name. But he hadn't forgotten. He even knew which breast he was going to cut. He marked it with a Sharpie Marker from the office supply department of K-Mart.

The anesthetic worked in such a way that I could be awake, but they promised me I would not remember it. Afterwards, Dr. Finn said I slept through the whole thing. Perhaps my snoring was a clever guise. I was not only awake, but I do remember. When Dr. Finn took out the actual tumor I could sense his relief that he had found it one unit, so to speak. I was really glad he was cheering for the patient to have an easy time, instead of looking for his own personal big surgical adventure.

I remember waiting, with the doctors and nurses for the lab report on the tumor. Then I remember the heavy tone of voice Dr. Finn had when he decided to go back "deeper." I knew he sincerely wanted me to recover as a human being, and not a piece of furniture. That gave me great hope. Then I felt like I was suffocating, and I tried to say that I could not breathe. The anesthesiologist performed more incantations with the instructions that I couldn't move. They held my arms. Again I said I couldn't breathe, but I couldn't talk either. Then I heard Dr. Finn give instructions to have the lab check the edges carefully. I knew it was safe to go to sleep.

When I awoke I was in the little curtained off booth in the out patient area. My husband came in. I was expecting the oncologist to be there because that was the prediction if I had cancer. Dr. Finn said, if it was malignant the oncologist would talk to me after the surgery. I was pretty sure it was cancer. But the only doctor who came in was Dr. Finn. With no frills, fringes or confusion he said, 2.8 cm of cancer cells were located in the center of the tumor. He believed he had gotten it all, but next they would take lymph nodes to see if it had spread. A follow-up appointment would be scheduled.

It was a relief to cry. It was actually a relief to have my fears confirmed about cancer, without hearing my worst fears confirmed about an imminent slow painful death. It was a relief to find Tom sitting there by me. He was not angry, or planning a divorce, or talking about money. He was just there, with tears too, offering with me a prayer. I was deeply grateful for this good fortune. But I didn't want to shout out in joy, "Thank you God for giving me a kind, loving understanding husband!" I kept that a silent prayer. Aloud that would only serve to level the responsibility of caring more heavily on his shoulders. I knew he must be feeling all those things he did not speak. "How we will pay for this?" "How will he come home to sickness day in and day out?" "How will he be alone as a father, mother, friend and pastor to our daughter?" "Who will be left to care for him?" But he did not say those things.

I was given a fat folder of brochures about different ways the hospital could deal with cancer patients. (That was a new self identity that was hard to grasp.) I was the "cancer patient." The first page was how to recover from this surgical procedure. And the last page was how Hospice can help families who lose someone to cancer. Another doctor's appointment was scheduled, and a nurse came in and took my I.V. out, so I could get dressed and go home.

The Telling

Who should know? We felt Mariah, being an only child and in a new high school, dealing with all those problems teens must face, needed to decide for herself who to tell, and who not to tell. In case she needed to confide in someone outside our home, we wanted to assure her she would not be going against our wishes.

Mariah has been endowed with the trendy academic label "Gifted and Talented." That opens the door for her to be in special programs at school, but it also lays the huge burden to "succeed" on her. So the day to day pressures for this teen were great, without having cancer looming over her threatening her mother's life, and perhaps lurking in her own genes. But the one real "gift" she had, that does not fit into any academic measurement or into any audition for talent, was her gift of a true spiritual perspective. She has an uncanny, and piercing ability to see herself in a realistic context with others, and to see psychological motivations, and spiritual truths as well. I always think Mariah sees from the vantage point of the angels. She is the first person I would trust to read my journal. But also, I know that she could make appropriate choices in sharing our family's sensitive issue with others. So we told her she did not have to be any more private about it than she felt she wanted to be.

But we chose not to tell the people of the church at that time because it might undermine Tom's ability to be available for the people in need of a pastor if they thought he was dealing with problems of his own. We decided to wait until the results of the lymph node surgery were in, then we would either be rejoicing, or everyone would be aware anyway as I went into more treatment or lost all my hair, or perhaps died or whatever.

Since it was the Christmas season, I had some responsibilities for hosting things at the parsonage which I could not postpone, so I did confide in one person, Betty, a school nurse, who was a friend and neighbor. I imagine in the depths of my secret consciousness I had hoped she might tell. I did what I could to start rumors. I felt I needed the sympathy. The party that was supposed to happen in the parsonage, happened. The church leaders, the Consistory, met at our house for Christmas dessert. Betty turned out to be a trusted friend who did not tell, so nothing dampened the spirit of the evening. She could also play the piano, so carols made the shadows into the holy night. The gathering of people celebrating the season brought a sense of warmth and joy to the whole house, that lingered throughout the season like embers in the fireplace.

We had held off writing Christmas letters, and making calls to friends and family, so that we could share good news with them of an unfounded cancer scare. But now we must choose the other words for our letters.

I thought about the members of our families, and pondered the various experiences with cancer that were part of this network already.

My father was a true "survivor." We had seen him off to cancer surgery several times, and he seemed to have no fear at all. He prayed, he told jokes, he laughed, he talked... he never cried. He had colon cancer many years ago, and had it completely removed surgically. Then he had a skin cancer removed, and he had, in the last few years, prostate cancer. He opted for surgery for that one too, since he had so much success with other surgery. Since he did not understand the value of radiation and he had a definite bias toward surgery, I knew Dad would be glad to know I was dealing with this surgically. I knew he would understand cancer, and talk with me reasonably about it, and would offer a source of hope and information.

My mother, on the other hand, had a very different attitude about cancer. Her mother died of cancer of the ear. That seems odd, but I have always known, since I was a young teen, that she died of a cancer caused by hormones. I believe that because every monthly cycle of hormones I experience I get an odd little dry skin infection in one or sometimes both ears. I have kept that information filed with my secret fears of family cancer along with my fear of medical devices. The only other cancer on my mother's side of the family was my cousin Gwen, who was my age and my best friend throughout my childhood. We were around forty when she died of a very aggressive form of breast cancer. She tried every possible treatment. She went from her home in Germany to the Mayo Clinic, near her family in Minnesota. She lost all her hair from some of the treatments, and died the traditional cancer death. My mother's family held out hope that if cancer was genetic, it was probably on her father's side, after all, Grandma Munro died of cancer of the ear, and who ever heard of that being inherited? It was a good thing Grandma Munro did not get breast cancer. She was a staunch believer in keeping secrets secret. Her personal modesty was impenetrable. She did not bare her breasts even to feed her babies and I am sure that the word "bosom" or any of its synonyms never passed between her lips.

Besides the dismal outcome of Munros with cancer, my mother had another characteristic that made me hope she wouldn't answer the phone when I called. She took every illness and every problem I ever had as her own personal struggle. Because of that little motherly trait she spent many more weeks in Hell than were required in a normal healthy life. I knew that if she knew I had cancer, she would say, why did it have to happen to her. And now, she actually was the mother of a cancer victim.

We called when we thought Dad would answer the phone. But Mom answered, and sure enough, she could not understand what she had done to elicit such a harsh judgment on herself. She was, however, prepared to deal with it, since she too had feared cancer most of her lifetime, and she had all those nine benign lumpectomies. (And that resolves the statistical issue.) She suggested books and tapes which she found useful in helping her fend off cancer until now, when I, the only irresponsible appendage of her body, got cancer. Since she read these books, and did not have cancer, she applied the concepts to cataract surgery which she did have. She asked me if I wanted her to call Bernie Siegel, who at that moment in time was a best selling author on cancer with his book, *Love, Medicine and Miracles*[3]. She wanted to call Dr. Siegel, because she had made a big painting for him, which illustrated her cataract. At her last art show she had this painting listed as "not for sale" in case there came the reason to give it to Dr. Siegel. She excitedly added that he only lives across the Sound in Connecticut. She could get there with a short ferry ride. I could come too, and he could tell me about breast cancer.

I knew this was her great opportunity to meet a famous cancer doctor who also wrote what she considered to be science books that did not discount the metaphysical. But I could not bring myself to soliciting more waiting rooms than were already before me. And I was not sure if my breast cancer really would be viewed by Dr. Siegel as the one great unique opportunity to study an actual case of breast cancer. I asked Mom to send me the book, and I would read it, and if I felt Dr. Siegel, cancer, me and my mom would all benefit from this proposed pilgrimage to Connecticut, I would be very grateful for her offer to barter her painting as a token of barter for my chance at life.

My call to Tom's mother was the easiest of all. I waited until I was alone the next morning, because I felt our conversation would only cause more stress for Tom. My mother in law, Lorena, was the one person I knew who had actually survived breast cancer, and she was a family member. Well, she was not a blood relative, but as in-laws go she was my very next of kin. Twenty years ago she had a double

---

[3]*Love, Medicine & Miracles -- Lessons Learned About Self-Healing from a Surgeon's Experience with Exceptional Patients* by Bernie S. Siegel, M.D., Harper & Row, Publishers, New York, 1986.

radical mastectomy. She had also had a radiation treatment on her eye, so I knew she knew what lay before me better than anyone else to whom I could talk. And the best part about it was that she was alive. We talked for a good half hour, and she confirmed my belief that, given the choice, surgery is the best way to cure cancer. She said her salvation came in the fact that "she caught it early." She had two different cancers. Both were in the early stages and had not spread to the lymph nodes. But she had to have both breasts removed because one cancer was in each breast. And she had to have lymph nodes removed too, to see if the cancer had spread. Certainly, now, twenty years later, they have found better ways to tell if it was spreading. I said, well, the doctor had said lymph node surgery was next. She said the recovery of the use of her arm was the hardest part. It took more than a year, and she had to wear an elastic stocking on her wrist to keep the swelling down, even though she was doing all the exercises that the volunteer from the American Cancer Society had explained to her.

When finally I called my parents back, Dad and Mom had already talked at length about my situation, and they had prayed about it. Dad could keep nothing else on his mind he said. I can imagine that Mom's dramatic style of presenting him with the news did not help either. He said he used to be able to think about several things at the same time, but now these deep concerns were a distraction. He said that day he did not have his mind on his driving. He was in an accident in which a child had been injured. He said he was thinking of giving up driving altogether. Dad did not make idle threats, so I knew he meant it. And yet his car, for him, was an extension of who he was. It symbolized his ability to get out and meet people. He could travel around and interview people for his newspaper column. He could work as an interim pastor, even though he was officially "retired." He could show up at the radio station early Sunday morning, for his little pastoral radio program, before he did his church service. His car let him do all these things he really loved to do.

The truth to tell, he was always having accidents. At least once in every decade of his life he had "totaled" a car. Old age was not a factor. Maybe he wasn't a "good" driver, but to give up driving due to old age was completely uncharacteristic of him. So I asked him not to be too rash. I suggested he try using the commuter train and the buses for a while until he could see forgiveness and grace more clearly and not be so harsh on himself. A few days later he reported giving that a try, and yes, he could work out transportation to his church which was fifty miles away by train.

But he and Mom had decided to buy a new car. And this car would be all Mom's. It would be her favorite color: teal blue. It would be small, and easy to handle. It would have every imaginable safety feature. And it would be a Saturn, because their advertising showed that the car was made by real, caring individuals. These down home people were talking safety, and Mom was listening. Mom would do all the driving, unless, of course, it was dark, or rainy, or icy. Then Dad, who is fearless and not distracted in the more challenging settings, would be the safest driver. It sounded like a plan they could agree on. It would also give them the freedom and independence they valued most.

We sent out Christmas cards, and started through the usual rituals of the season. But with each twinge of the pain of my recovering breast, was also the pain of knowing I must be prepared to separate myself from this physical life. Setting up a Christmas tree hurts. Thinking it may be the last Christmas tree was very painful. Hanging ornaments, rolling out cookies, wrapping gifts, playing Christmas carols on the guitar all were painful. All the good things were cause for grief and sadness. Up was down, and down was up. Would I ever smell this fragrance of the pine and the bayberry again? Was this to be my last celebration with my family?

All of the symbols of the holy season define this very moment when the boundary between the physical and the spiritual, and between the profane and the holy becomes narrow and clouded. The manifestation of God on earth was the mirror image of my feelings at this time. That is to say, Christmas felt backwards.

Reading Up

In the days to come I read the pamphlets supplied by the hospital, most of which were published by the National Cancer Institute.[4] They were carefully worded so that the reader would not learn anything he or she was not ready to hear. Every real question I had was asked, but then answered with "Your doctor will tell you." So I went to the library, since I wanted to hear all the answers to my questions while I was alone, not spoken at me by a doctor. Books kept me from having the hear bad news from real people. I could read ahead, and know what was coming. I could cry ahead, and pray ahead. I wanted to know everything before it was spoken aloud so I could be in control. I sort of wanted to approach cancer pre-prayed.

---

[4]The National Cancer Institute has a toll free number: 1-800-4-CANCER. The American Cancer Society has the toll free number: 1-800-ACS-2345

There were lots of cancer books on the library shelves and in book stores, and health food stores. Breast cancer was especially well documented. I found answers to everything I was asking in the books. I could even find definitive answers about scientific causes and cures for cancer, which I happen to know really don't exist. But in books you can find anything. The health food store's books cured cancer with diet. So I followed those instructions. I was already a health food fanatic, so I knew in my heart that if it really was diet, I never would have gotten cancer at all. But it was an easy fix, and since I was already trying the hard fixes like the medical stuff, I should also try the easy fixes. It was something to do. I read about prayer for healing, and again, prayer was already a basic part of my life. But I stuck with it any way. I read about breathing deeply, and exercising . So I tried to do those things.

 The scientific information was the most useful of all, but I found I had to arrange the books in a stack with the straight science on the bottom, and the easy, lay person's books and pamphlets on the top. Then I went through the stack with one question in mind, I found that answer, and then I attacked the altar of information with another query. Over and over again I tackled the pile of books until I knew more than I ever knew anyone would ever want to know about breast cancer.

I was very curious to know what kind of cancer cells the biopsy found, and if the lab had tested for various things about which I read. I learned the blood test they did CA27-29 was a very new test for a certain protein in the blood thought to be produced by a present tumor. The test was defined as a tumor marker. I learned that premenopausal breast cancer, such as I had, was likely to be the fast spreading type that was especially deadly and the dreaded chemotherapy was, according to some sources, the only real hope. I read that there were two usual groups of drugs given in chemotherapy depending on the stage of breast cancer: CMF and CAF. The CAF is the stronger of the two, and definitely causes hair loss, and all that other stuff that gives chemotherapy a bad name.

I could see then, that if my lymph nodes were positive, I would have "advanced cancer," and would need chemotherapy for sure, and it would probably be CAF. If they were not positive, the safest plan would be chemotherapy, but CMF would do. Most everything was recommending radiation, or a complete radical mastectomy. So I knew that my follow up visit to Dr. Finn would probably include some of this information and an appointment to see someone who was something other than the surgeon, like a chemotherapy, or medical oncologist, or radiation oncologist.

By the time of my appointment with Dr. Finn, just a week after the lump surgery, I had been to the library for several helpings of books. I was half way through this self-imposed medical school. What I lost in breast tissue, I made up in scientific knowledge. I was amazed Dr. Finn recognized me at all, the changed person that I was. He not only remembered me, though, he remembered my ignorance and phobias. He very gently talked about my next surgery to remove axillary nodes, as though I had no idea of what was going on. He talked about the grueling side effects of having impaired channels for lymph to follow, and the possibility that he would have to cut the main nerve that goes through part of my arm, leaving me with a permanent numbness in my right arm. A permanent numbness in my arm is a small price for healing from this disease that could cause the big eternal numbness. He could see he hadn't frightened me yet.

I asked, "what happens then, after the lymph node surgery." Dr. Finn went into his very serious mode and looked away from me, and then started listing every imaginable cancer horror I had ever heard: chemotherapy, radiation, and probably more surgery to put a device in my main vein to give me a permanent I.V port. That was scarier than anything I had even read about yet. It sounded to me like the proverbial "fate worse than death." This is the very thing I had feared most— becoming a piece of medical equipment. And they could really do that to me. So, looking for an easy out I asked, "what about death. If I do all this stuff is it likely that I will live?" Dr. Finn assured me they didn't have enough information to answer a question like that. I didn't feel assured. He said he knew a nurse who had chemotherapy and she lived, and even became a mother. Gee, that was not on my agenda at all. But I know he meant to be offering hope. He gave me the name of the oncologist I was going to be seeing, Dr. Apple. But the place in the conversation, "which do you prefer: surgery, radiation, or chemotherapy?" never came up. I was prepared to answer "surgery." But I never felt like I had that option.

I really wanted to meet the assigned oncologist, Dr. Apple, in his/her office when I was in my normal state of wellness, so he (or perhaps she) could get a mental picture of me as a normal person, not just a "cancer patient." That meant a lot to me. I called my insurance to see if they would pay for a pre-treatment office visit. They said of course. So I called Dr. Apple for an appointment. After two long conversations with the receptionist I finally understood, Dr. Apple does not see normal people. He only sees cancer patients. So, I sent him a note, with my picture, and in the picture was also my husband and my daughter. I was hoping that would keep my humanity in perspective with my disease. I did not get an answer from Dr. Apple.

The book and audio tapes of the book arrived from Mom in the mail, along with a gift of a pillow. I wondered if she realized I was still walking around, doing things, looking for all the world, like a normal healthy person. Certainly I would be getting hand embroidered hospital gowns and hand painted bedpans for Christmas if I did not let her know. So we made plans to get together on Christmas day. Since both my dad and my husband were pastors, and Christmas Eve being a big church time, we rarely celebrated Christmas together, but this year it seemed very important to do that.

I listened to Bernie Siegel on the tape talk about "good"[5] cancer patients, distinguishing them from survivors. And people who survived seemed to be the ones who gave the doctors the hardest time. They asked questions. They had a stake in controlling their illness. Just in the brief experience I had into the world of what doctors tell, I could well understand that. He went on to talk about the cancer personality— The voice on the tape buzzed through a list of features common to cancer patient. The tape blipped. I popped it out to see what was wrong. The tape was stretched out and worn right in that spot that so perfectly describes my father, my grandmother, my cousin and me. Obviously, Mom had turned it off and just let it sit in the tape player when the message started hitting too close to home even though some of the characteristics that were listed were not things that were usually considered to be faults. Could it be that the very thing that we call righteousness in our lives of faith, is really our sin for which cancer is the consequences? This explains the pavement of "good intentions" on the road to Hell.

---

[5]Dr. Siegle explains in his book, *Love, Medicine and Miracles* that in this explanation a "good" patient is one who is, among other things, a "submissive, sufferer."

CHAPTER 2

The Christmas Celebration

 hristmas came, and Tom and Mariah and I went to Long Island as planned. My brother Jack came out from Michigan, so our whole family, all six of us, had gathered at Mom and Dad's house way out on the end of Long Island, by the ocean.

Mom always served Rock Cornish hens and green and white Jello for these special occasions, and for dessert we inevitably had pecan pie or brownies. The Cornish hens represented one of those great old family traditions. The other entrees simply reflected Mom's limited repertoire of celebration food.

When Jack and I were children, Dad changed from being a rural pastor in Central Illinois, to being an executive for the National Council of Churches, which had just moved to the brand new Inter Church Center on Riverside Drive in New York City. That meant our family had to move to the New York area. We found a house in the newly developing suburban city of Massapequa Park, on the south shore of Long Island. Our mid-western twang had all the "r"s in different places than Long Islanders had ever heard. Some thought we were from the South. Others figured we must be Nazi's because our last name was German in origin, and we ate bacon, so we surely were not Jewish. Some people couldn't understand us at all.

In our yearnings for a homeland, in rural Illinois, I decided to become a cowboy, perhaps in another century, while my brother set his sights more realistically on becoming a present day farmer. Mom and Dad wanted to nurture Jack's development as a farmer so they smuggled some tiny baby chicks into our suburban home. They were special chicks, so they wouldn't seem so farmish. Nevertheless, chickens are livestock, not pets, and livestock was not allowed in the suburbs, so the chicks spent most of their feather growing days in the basement. Then as they got older, even though they were unusually tiny for chickens, it was clear they had to have a little outdoor time every now and then. Dressing them up as acceptable pets like parakeets or dogs was impractical. So we just tried to keep them hidden.

They became a bigger and bigger detriment to our tranquility. I think the last straw for my mother (who was a city girl, and not at all a farmer) was when the chickens got soused. I had collected a box of empty wine bottles in the basement to be made into candle holders for a party. A little wine spilled out onto the basement floor, and the chickens imbibed.   Drunk chickens are chickens that know no fear. They were a whole new bird in fact. Drunk chickens make worse pets than sober chickens. So, Dad, who really had been raised on a farm, knew just what to do.

We have always had Rock Cornish hen for holidays ever since, so that no one will ever know when the particular Rock Cornish hens who had names, and lived with us, were actually being served. At this family get together the chicken story did not even have to be spoken aloud. We already all knew it. The menu was just as expected, and just as it should be.

We did not talk about our fears either, we talked about our dreams: the possibilities for Jack's growing business, Mom's artwork, Mariah's college search, Dad's newspaper column, Tom's church work, my plans for a garden next year. More than dreams, they were our hopes. We each had a secret understanding that this would be our last time together, and all the words we needed to say had been accomplished on the telephone. We did not talk out loud about our fears. Yet the prayer at the table included the words, "The hopes and fears for all the years, are met in Thee, tonight.[6]"

The next morning I hugged my mom and dad and brother, as we got in the car to leave. Like the moment before the applause, when you realize this is the curtain call, and you ponder the evaluation: "it was a very good time."

Dreams and an Opinion

January, 1997

The lymph node (axillary) surgery was scheduled in January, after the Christmas vacation. A couple of days before that medical event I dreamed that I was in that dull green hospital holding pen for surgery patients, on a gurney, expecting to see Dr. Finn stop in to assure me he knew my name, and which arm he would be cutting. Instead, Dan Ackroyd and John Belushi ("The Blues Brothers" from movies and T.V.) stopped by. Then I was wheeled into surgery. Still, there was no Dr. Finn. Just the Blue's Brothers were there, and it looked like they were getting ready to operate. I asked "so where's Dr. Finn?" They told me he had traded jobs with the Blues Brothers temporarily, to see how it would be to take on a new role. John Belushi (who actually was deceased at the time of this dream and this writing), announced "we are

---

[6]From the carol, "O Little Town of Bethlehem" by Phillips Brooks, 1868.

musicians, not physicians!" I thought of Dr. Finn on stage, trying to be a comedian. A sense of horror came over me. If Dr. Finn is so ill-suited for stand-up comedy, what must the Blue's Brothers be like as surgeons?

Tom told me not to tell Dr. Finn about this dream. So, I did not. I did not tell Dr. Finn even in the surgery storage room, after I knew I was safe because it was him (and not the Blues Brothers) who came in, and he remembered my name. Then the nurse came in to stick the I.V. needle in my hand. She was the same nurse who one month earlier had received the call about her child's head injury. To distract myself I asked her how her child was doing. She was amazed I remembered, she said her child was fine. Suddenly we were talking as human beings, not as nurse, and hospital item. So I happened to tell her I had a dream where Dr. Finn traded places with The Blues Brothers, and Dr. Finn was not a very good comedian. She could not resist telling the anesthesiologist who not only administers hallucinogens but he also may have been The Blues Brothers best living fan. He knew their routines by heart, or memory, or whatever one uses to make eternal the mortal words. He enjoyed repeating, "we are musicians, we are not physicians," and as I was drifting off I remember, Dr. Finn came in and heard the anesthesiologist's strange chant, and that is how Dr. Finn heard the story, but I did not tell him.

The recovery room was crowded. I could hear myself screaming, and I knew if I was only awake I would be able to move and make the tingling in my arm better. But I heard Dr. Finn and I think, the anesthesiologist talking, and they decided to give me "morphine." That is actually what they called it. I was surprised they didn't have a secret medical name for it. I stopped screaming.

The hospital stay was the Insurance Company blue plate special called a "23 hour short stay." "Short stays" happen in an "outpatient" area. This was the latest thing in hospital progress. It was so new in fact, that the outpatient nurses didn't seem to know anything about my type of surgery. They only knew what was written on the chart, and that's what they did. Every two hours an aid came and checked my blood pressure, temperature, and I.V. Every two hours I asked, "is it going to hurt anything if I move my arm?" And, "May I have a smaller water glass?" But no one could answer any questions. Every two hours the nurse or the aid left the room saying, "I don't know, I'll find out." But no one ever did. No one knew if I was supposed to have meals so they did not bring meals.

I found that years of strength and health paid off, because I could sit up, without using my arms. Therefore I could get up to use the bathroom because that did not require bending my arms. With cut nerve and drainage tubes in one arm, and an I.V. in the other, I couldn't reach the phone, the call button, the water cup or even move the blanket unless I got completely out of bed, and it was a very high leap to the floor. Since no one could figure out if I was actually allowed to get up, I just did.

Finally my request for a smaller water cup got a response. One nurse's aid finally got through the whole chain of command and learned that I could not have a smaller glass because they were supposed to measure how much water I drank, and a smaller cup would be too confusing. The large quart sized glass was not the least bit confusing. Not a drop was missing when they measured it, because I couldn't lift it.

I never did get the surgical gown off and the hospital gown on until Dr. Finn came in the next morning and checked the bandages and asked why I was still wearing the heavy green gown. Then he also found that the big pain in the middle of my back that I thought must be some cut muscle or something was a blister from the bandage. That bandage blister took more healing trouble and left a worse scar than the surgeries.

This outpatient surgery for breast cancer was a regular story in the news that month. It seems insurance companies were dictating to doctors that mastectomies had to be done as outpatient surgery. And doctors were complaining about it. The newsies catch phrase for it was, "drive through mastectomy." Every news program included an interview with some poor hairless round faced woman in a bed, saying how hard it was to be sent home after this surgery. My assessment of the situation was that home would be a big improvement. The shorter the stay the better. At home I would not be so far from the floor. The I.V. wouldn't be there. I could go to the refrigerator and get something to eat. I could drink water from any sized glass I chose, and I could wear clothes. If any bad medical thing happened I could reach the telephone or call Tom at the church. In the hospital, I could not reach the phone, or the call button. So if I had needed anything there, it wouldn't have mattered. My short stay taught me, no stay is best.

Dr. Finn told me he thought he may have seen a positive lymph node, but the lab report would tell. He was sure he took out plenty of non-cancerous lymph nodes, so they weren't all affected. He was sure of that. He said Dr. Apple was coming in to talk to me. And that day, just before Tom took me home, Dr. Apple did stop in. I was really pleased I had gotten dressed before this meeting, so that I could look a little less victimized by the disease. Dr. Apple was a stocky light-haired man, perhaps in his late forties. He was wearing a tan blazer, which I took as an intentional gesture not to frighten me with a medical presence. He carried a clip-board. Perhaps it was blank. Or possibly, it told all the secrets of my chances to survive this. He asked me the familiar list of questions and marked off items on the clipboard as he went.

As I left the hospital that day, we passed a nurses' station where Dr. Apple, and a tall, dark haired woman physician were looking something up in a huge book — it reminded me of the automotive service manuals my brother used as an auto-mechanic. I always trust a mechanic who uses the service manual after all, there is a great deal to be said for literacy among auto mechanics. I felt very safe. Doctors had a service manual, that meant, they could, possibly get things right. And at last I had permission to call and make an appointment to see Dr. Apple in his office.

Diagnosis

The appointment with Dr. Apple began with the usual examination. He saw my newly formed breast, and commented that "some ladies" were not as fortunate as I was. They have considerably more disfigurement. I tried to overlook his use of the word "ladies" to classify my gender, but it definitely struck my feminist cord. Lying on a table, with my clothing stripped away, and a man feeling my breasts, I was in no position to think about insensitivity. I tried to agree. "It seems to have a more youthful contour."

I thought about "ladies." People rarely use that word any more, except as a label on a bathroom that has no urinal. I haven't really aspired to be a "lady" since our high school gym class lesson on sitting with knees together while wearing a miniskirt.

Maybe Dr. Apple, being from this Pennsylvania German community just grew up with that word and he meant it respectfully. Maybe when he was a small child classifying women as "ladies" was normal and he just never let it go as times changed.

I could imagine a little Dr. Apple sitting in a play pen in the church basement, while the "Ladies' Aid" — the predecessor of the Church Women's Group, had quilting and sewing. My mother, and maybe Dr. Apple's mother went to these daytime gatherings where women of the churches all across the country produced various needed items for charity. My mother was always in groups that worked on "Cancer pads" and "Cancer wrappings." These projects were, I think, holdovers from war times when women tore bandages for the wounded. But in my lifetime, and in Dr. Apple's day as well, the blank faced needy were no longer the war wounded. So the victims in the cancer wards filled that role. Maybe Dr. Apple's lifetime of service as a doctor was shaped by the compassion he felt, as he waited in that play pen for his mother — who was certainly a lady, while she sacrificially gave her time to produce cancer pads. Okay. I could live with the idea that he called people of my gender "ladies."

Tom was then escorted into the examining room for our conversation about treatment. As soon as Tom sat down, Dr. Apple shifted from talking to me, to talking to Tom about me. Again, I was aware of his tendency to regard my gender, or perhaps just me, as secondary.

This was a marathon monologue of science words. I understood some, and recognized that he was also explaining a lot in "layman's terms" — So it was a little confusing to try to sort the science from the down to earth explanation. I clearly heard him say, "There are some very good things, and there are some very bad things, and some things are in between." I agreed with him. And I could see Tom nodding agreement at this also. I knew if anyone would understand that some things are very good, and some things are very bad, and some things are in between, it would be Tom, because Tom is very wise. Dr. Apple went on to say, "Of course more will have to be known, and we don't know a lot." That part was also quite clear. But then, I already knew that the knowledge of cancer is not complete.

Then we listened to his plan for treatment. He talked about various drugs and their effects. But I really couldn't figure out from what he said if he was thinking I would have the CAF or the CMF about which I had read, or something completely different, and mysteriously new.

I thought I could focus this question without sounding like I had read more books than a non-scientist was privy to, by asking, "will I loose all of my hair?" He answered, "Oh, we don't know how any one person will respond to these drugs. Probably your hair will just thin out a little. Now, the breast cancer drugs we give to the young ladies, yes, they do lose all their hair with those."

I thought, oh good, they decided I was a Stage I or II, in the "early stages," and I will only have to have the CMF drugs. I was very hopeful.

The plan was to have chemo and radiation at the same time. So the next step was to make an appointment with Dr. Tallhouse, the radiation oncologist.

January was blending to February when I finally got in to see Dr. Tallhouse. He was the youthful, curly haired doctor that casting directors try to duplicate, but actors really don't come with that piercing bare-naked truth scientific style, no matter how hard they practice in front of a mirror.

Dr. Tallhouse peered over his huge doctor desk, and asked, "So what did Dr. Apple tell you?"

I answered, "He said I would need radiation and chemo at the same time, then five years of Tamoxifen. I really liked the part about the five years. I think he thinks I will be here five years from now."

Dr. Tallhouse looked away and said "He does? Did he tell you that these undifferentiated cells mean a very aggressive type of cancer? Did he tell you what the clump of lymph nodes means?"

This sounded like the stuff I had read in books, but not like what Dr. Apple was talking about, unless it was what he meant in the "there are some very bad things." I told Dr. Tallhouse that I had been reading about breast cancer, and I knew there were four stages, but I couldn't figure out what stage my cancer would be considered to be.

"You are listed as Stage III, and that is an advanced stage of the disease. Maybe you are Stage IV. We haven't seen the results of a bone scan or even an X-Ray to know if it has spread further. When are you having those tests done?"

"I don't know." I looked at Tom. He looked a thousand years old. I thought he would be angry with Dr. Tallhouse for being so blunt. But he wasn't angry. He just shared my complete disappointment.

Dr. Tallhouse asked me what I knew of the treatment that was planned. I told him I was pretty sure Dr. Apple planned CMF, because he said he didn't think I would lose all my hair.

He said, "Why CMF? Why not CAF? You have a sixteen year old daughter. Do you want to see her graduate from high school? If I were you I would be looking into every possible protocol." He said his recommendation was to wait with radiation until after I am done with chemo, because the chemo that is weak enough to do simultaneously with radiation, is too weak.

We were very disappointed. I had my appointment to start chemo coming up in just a week, and I did not want to delay treatment any longer. Yet I felt that I needed to get the tests Dr. Tallhouse recommended, and I wanted to get a second opinion. I had no idea of how to go about that. But I definitely wanted to see Mariah graduate from high school. That was my secret hope that I was afraid to say aloud, for fear a doctor would say, "no way." And Dr. Tallhouse, who knows nothing of me but what is in my medical records pinpointed that one hope I was secretly nurturing.

Feb. 97

A Second Opinion

Science is great. It finds cures for diseases. It gives us tools to look into the heavens and marvel at the vastness of the universe. It is even credited with the creation of "spell check." I am constantly amazed at what science has accomplished for human beings. But science is not really all there is. It is a method of learning the truths of the creation. It is not our creator. Science is merely one way of gathering information.

When I hear of families who have allowed a child to die because they choose not to use modern medicine in order to use purely faith healing, I am very sad. I am sad for the child and for the parents who miss the benefits that a scientific perspective has to offer, but also, I am sad for our society which accuses the parents of abusing the child because they placed their faith in things unseen instead of science. We do not bring parents to trial when medical technology fails, accusing them of abuse because they did not pray for their child. Is that not the same issue? Prayer (or more broadly meditation) is often considered a factor in healing.[7] So, is omitting prayer from the care of a sick child not, also, to be considered abuse in the same way as omitting modern medical procedures? Or has science secretly become our national religion?

If science is a way of gaining understanding it is valuable. If faith in modern science and technology is an alternative to faith in God, it is a very dismal error. That which is eternal was, and is and will be, beyond all of mortal Creation and certainly beyond human knowledge of Creation. That's a really hard concept to grasp from within a body, holding a pen, with tangible substance all around us, but it is true. If we could separate the physical world from the spiritual world, as in some strange Gnostic laboratory experiment we would see that reality falls on the side of the spiritual. The physical state is actually the miraculous or the supernatural. That which we call Creation, the tangible world, is like a poem constructed of metaphor, which God has given so that we

---

[7]Helpful advice on meditation and healing is offered in various sources. I found particularly helpful, Bernie Siegel's book, *Love, Medicine & Miracles*, and also *Cancer as a Turning Point A Handbook for People with Cancer, Their Families, and Health Professionals*, by Lawrence LeShan, Ph.D., Plume, Penguin Books, New York Copyright © 1989.

might know the spiritual nature of God. Why is that so amazing? Of course isolating the "spiritual world" into one realm and the "physical" into another forces an artificial duality that is not real either.

We started thinking that reality was purely physical, maybe about 500 years ago, in a time called "The Age of Enlightenment," when a round world was conceivable. Science came into power with the notion that reality is defined by only the five physical senses, all of them located on the physical face of a human being. Dog whistles and miracles are not topics for science. To speak of anything beyond human physical sensitivity it must be translated, or reinterpreted to make sound, or be visible, or tangible or odorous, or tasty, or else science must conclude it does not exist.

Limiting human knowledge to just what can be perceived through the five senses of the human face solved the problem medieval artists were having in painting Heaven and Hell. If you can't perceive it optically, you can't paint it. So they did stop painting it for a few eras of art, then science created hallucinogens, so artists could again visualize Hell.

Now, one would think that painting only what can be seen would have simplified the task of the late gothic artists, but new rules called, ironically enough, "perspective" came along, and it was perfectly clear that a picture of reality must have a mathematical distortion in order to "look real." With the use of a "vanishing point" and a horizon, images could be angularly distorted to look more realistic.

While art had its open ended question solved, science opened some other gapping ends and beginnings too. If all that is reality is that which is perceivable by the human head (touch, smell, vision, auditory sense, or taste), then how can things beyond the human dimension be explained? Or, is there anything beyond the human face?

What about life before the world began? Or what about life after physical death? What about life at all? We believe in it because it can be measure by the sound of a heart beat, or the view of blips on a screen. But without science how would we know we were alive? And what about God? If God is as big as God would need to be to do what God does, then how could the human face perceive it?

Over and over again, God reduces that answer to print on a page. Over and over again, God speaks to us in small human ways we can understand. We have our faith books, and our prophets in each religious background. If we are part of an illiterate culture God speaks in the voices of our grandmothers and grandfathers, or in signs and symbols of nature. God's presence is known to us. We have to learn to close God out if we want to be without God in our lives. Children know God. It takes an intentional turning away to not know God.

Where did beauty come from? What is music? Why does music grow plants and give us peace? How does the sun shine? Why can we see the stars through our earth's dense atmosphere? Who thought of growing? Why do we get healed? Why don't we have a cure for colds and cancer? How do people get better if science has no cure? What if reality is spiritual and physical things (even including the five senses of the human head) are merely miraculous manifestations of the spiritual reality, like the vanishing point on a horizon in a gothic painting?

Reading about things of science, the gnosis (secret knowledge) of medicine gives clues about doctors. Doctors are actually human beings. They have this impossible task of telling people what they don't ever want to hear, while at the same time, making what they say no longer true. Three doctors have looked at the same data, and drawn the same conclusion, that I have Stage III Breast Cancer. And yet I felt they were telling me vastly different things. The problem is, doctors keep acting like human beings. I always thought the problem would be that doctors did not act like human beings. But that is not the problem at all.

Dr. Tallhouse said he would talk to Dr. Apple about changing my course of treatment so I would not have radiation and chemo simultaneously. He said Dr. Apple would call me and talk with me further about that. Dr. Apple did not call. At 7:30 the next morning Dr. Tallhouse called in person, not through a receptionist. He explained that radiation would be scheduled to follow chemo treatment. I was very relieved to know that someone in the field of medicine was concerned.

I scheduled the appointment for the bone scan that week, and my dentist was trying to get whatever I needed done for the coming months done so my teeth would not be a possible source of infection if the chemo weakened my immune system. So on the day of my scheduled appointment with Dr. Apple I had just had the injection of nuclear stuff to prepare for the bone scan, and I had two days of novocaine at the dentist. I thought I was going to the hospital's Medical Oncology Unit to get the lay of the land, and see what chemotherapy actually entailed. I thought Dr. Apple would tell me about the conversation he had with Dr. Tallhouse, and he would lay out the new plan for me. While I was waiting to see the doctor the nurse took my blood for the CA27-29 test. And as I talked with her, I realized Dr. Apple was planning my treatment to begin that very day! The nurse, seemed to agree that I would not want to start chemo while I was having dental work done, and while I was having nuclear medicine for the bone scan. So, when Dr. Apple came in, and realized I was not planning to have a treatment, I felt I could be firm about setting a new starting date. He said we had already talked, and we did not need to waste time talking any more.

I asked the nurse what were my chances to get done with cancer and still live. She went to the computer to read my chart then came back. "If you don't have treatment you have a very small chance of survival. With chemotherapy your chances for five year survival are considered 50/50." That was great news. My imagined fears never get anything so evenly in my favor.

I found out exactly how to go about getting a second opinion. The fierce competition for health money has cancer centers advertising on T.V. So, I copied phone numbers off the screen, and called two in the Philadelphia area. The first one wanted my insurance information, and no questions or details about my health. The second one had a nurse who would answer my health questions before they checked on my insurance. I chose the second place because someone was willing to talk to me before I paid a bill. But evidently the first cancer center I had called really did need me, since a month or so later it was announced that hospital was undergoing a reorganization process to solve its financial woes.

At the big central Philly Cancer Hospital, it was, as promised in the ads, a team of cancer specialists. I was assigned to a woman oncologist, Dr. Johnson. I tried to pretend that it did not matter if the doctor was a man or woman. I tried to convince myself that the gender of the doctor had nothing to do with me. But it was much more comfortable to think of my life in the hands of a woman.

I made a bunch of phone calls to the local hospital that had my records to collect everything the Philly hospital said they needed. My chemo was scheduled to begin the following Wednesday, so if I wanted to choose a different course of treatment I had Monday and Tuesday to do it. The Cancer Center obliged, and I got in on Monday.

On that day we stopped at the local hospital to pick up all of my records, to take with us. Then Tom drove on to Philly for our first visit to the city since we had moved to Pennsylvania. I peeked in the envelope of medical records, as though I was snooping into some highly confidential file. The thought never really crossed my mind that I was actually allowed to look at my own medical records.

The first thing was a report of my bone scan. I could see plainly, that it said I did not have cancer in my bones. That was the very first good medical news I had ever gotten. I felt like calling everyone and telling them! I felt completely invincible. The word "hope" seemed shallow. I started thinking in "plans."

We allowed two hours in which to get lost, but we didn't get lost. So we had two hours to wait in the waiting room. We watched the "city" all within the context of a cancer center. People in all sizes, shapes and colors filed by, each with no hair, each walking slowly to the reception desk. The decor was modern, clean and fast, but the corners showed urban wear. Even the magazines in the rack were worn to shreds despite the protective plastic covers.

I imagined myself in that line of patients at the desk. I realized I could choose to be here, or not. Having a choice about whether to come here or not, also meant I had a choice about going to the local hospital, and following Dr. Apple's plan. Whatever I decided to do from here on would be my choice. That was a great feeling of fearless control.

The first doctor we saw was Dr. Abram. He was kind, thorough, and the first doctor that both Tom and I liked. Dr. Johnson reviewed my records while Dr. Abram examined me, and talked with me.

Dr. Abram absolved me of my big cancer sin. He said that this kind of cancer that I have is a very aggressive, rapidly spreading type. He explained that I have probably only had it for six months. It was actually about six months before that day that I had first been aware of it. He explained that a regular mammogram could miss it for that reason.

Then Dr. Johnson came in and talked with me further. The bottom line was still the same. I had Stage III-A breast cancer. My choices of treatment were the standard CAF chemotherapy, or a bone marrow transplant in a clinical trial. That was the only clinical trial for which I qualified, that they offered at that cancer center.

I asked what was involved in that. I learned that basically, in my kind of case, they would use my own bone marrow, or stem cells, for making blood cells, and would first remove them, then they could give me very strong chemotherapy, and then put the stem cells back so I could regain the use of my immune system. I asked "what if I am allergic to chemotherapy?" They said that was a risk. I thought, I would like to try small doses, before I get into it so far. Those kinds of thoughts are so un-medical, I didn't even bother to share it. I asked, what if I have standard chemo now, can I get the stem cell transplant later? Dr. Abram explained that the A in CAF is adrymycin which builds up over use in the heart, and never goes away. So repeating chemo treatment more than three times is not done. I took that as a "yes." I can do both, but not lots of times.

The other issue here was that a clinical trial is not necessarily covered by my insurance. I had heard a rumor that it could cost as much as one hundred and forty thousand dollars. That would buy Tom a lifetime of Saabs, his dream car. It would buy a house, or a college education for Mariah and a wardrobe for her to wear to class. It may, or may not buy me a chance to live. And if I lived, I would never be able to find a job where I could pay the debt back in time for Mariah's college.

But I now had a choice. I was really hoping the choice would be between chemo therapy or some clinical trial to see if humor cures cancer. I could have my treatment by watching cartoons, and reading funny stories. Or perhaps it could have been a choice between chemo or an aroma-therapy experiment. I would be glad to be the first to find out that smelling mint and basil potpourri would cure cancer. The clinical trial bone marrow transplant seemed like it was so "clinical" and so much of a "trial."

So I asked specifics about standard chemo. I learned that it is basically the same at the local hospital as it is at this cancer center. The big difference I could see was that the facility was more crowded, and the ride home longer from Philadelphia. On the other hand, I really liked these city doctors. Now I had actual choices. I could weigh all the options and make a rational decision.

I chose to go ahead as planned, and start my treatment on Wednesday at the hospital nearer my home. I would want assurances that I was getting the three drugs in CAF. I felt that this would be the "best thing." With the possibility that if this didn't work perhaps it would at least buy me enough time that the stem cell transplant would be more widely available. And it would also give me a chance to find out what chemo therapy is really like for me.

William Faulkner's story "Old Man"[8] aired on T.V. that evening, as I pondered the options. It was a story about choices. A young man, a prison trustee, was offered every possible opening to his freedom. He was offered earthly options like being let out of prison, and spiritual options, like baptism and death. He chose to serve his prison time, and become an old man before starting his life. That is what I have done isn't it? I have chosen to cling to life as I know it.

It is amazing how consistently and confidently an entire community of knowledge (i.e. medicine) can say "This is the right thing to do, since we don't know what we are doing anyway."

While I had the microscope slides and all the medical records at home and in my hands that night, I became more and more curious about the information they contained. Finally my good manners gave way to my curiosity, and I pulled everything out of the envelope to see what doctors saw. There were lots of reports, beginning with one that called me a "well developed adult female." and there were microscope slides. These were actual cancer -- my cancer. I went down to the basement to the collection of old toys leftover from

---

[8]*Three Famous Short Novels*, by William Faulkner, Vintage Books, New York, Copyright © 1961.

Mariah's childhood. The Fisher Price plastic microscope needed a battery, so I raided a flashlight. I looked at the pathology slides with the toy microscope. It was very clear, and very interesting. I could look eye to eye with this mysterious enemy. I could clearly see the flat cells that the accompanying report identified as breast cells, and I could also see other shapes of tan colored cells the pathologist described as cancer. I saw all sizes of those, and I could see how they spread around. Tan is such a boring color. I kind of thought something this deadly would be chartreuse, or at least some variety of scarlet. I took a peak, then I put everything back, just as though no one but doctors had ever looked inside the envelope.

The Living Room--Room for Living

Now in this dream there are two areas in a large room separated by a divider counter, about 4 feet high. I could see over it, and taller people could reach across, or use it as a counter top. The people within the barrier are laughing and eating. They have a computer with a screen saver with dancing cartoons, and bleeping sounds. Phones are ringing. Lots is happening. On the side of the wall where I seem to be, there are chairs in a line and people waiting. The people in the chairs are reading thick books. But each has only a few printed pages, before the ending sections in the books which are reams of blank pages. Some people's books have blank pages starting in the middle, and going to the end, others were already near the end of their books with only a few blank pages. I had this very journal with me, and a pen. I had many blank pages also. Just like them.

In this dream, I was trying to get the attention of the people at the desk behind the barrier. I wanted to tell them that my book was different because it was a journal, and it was still being written. The blank pages in my book were not an end, but they were my future. I tried to shout over the bleeping of the computer. Finally someone heard me, and smiled as I explained my book. I thought surely she understood. Then she said "Just sit down in the chairs out there. Everybody has a book."

The first Wednesday in February Tom went with me to the real life setting for that dream. The M.O.U. (Medical Oncology Unit) at the local Hospital. I had the house clean, and the refrigerator filled with applesauce, jello and juice. I was ready to begin.

Dr. Apple knew I went to get a second opinion. He knew Dr. Tallhouse wanted a different treatment plan than he had prescribed. I wanted to explain that he did not call me back, or answer my calls or my questions. But more than that I wanted to know what was going to happen next. So I listened carefully to his explanation. He was being paged over the loudspeaker. But he did not answer the page. He stayed and talked to me. I know he was trying to give me his best, after all the mind changing and treatment shopping. I wanted to say, "The problem is, someone is paging you... What if that was me?" But I also had another question: "Who could I call if I had a problem?" He said "Call me, or you can call here. Laura will give you instructions."

He was very adamant. Do not call your family doctor. Do not call any other doctor. You may call this Dr. Williams, and she may have no idea that you are receiving chemotherapy, and your symptoms may sound like the flu to her, and she may prescribe something that will be the wrong thing. So only call me, or this M.O.U. I am your doctor now.

That was scary. Dr. Williams's number is on our speed dial on our telephone. Dr. Williams is well-known as a doctor who listens to questions. She calls back. She sees me in town, at the grocery store and she asks how I am. I trust Dr. Williams.

Dr. Apple was clearly getting annoyed with my string of questions. I wanted to hear him explain what I had read in pamphlets — that if I had this symptom I would have this medicine, etc. etc. Finally he said, you are probably the kind of person who sits down and reads all those manuals when you get a new car. Oh, yes! I am. My mind flashed back to the tall dark haired doctor at the nurses station reading the large manual.

Dr. Apple left and Laura came in and took out an arsenal of needles and plastic bags. She took the strange colored liquids and hung them over my head, then she took a viney strange medical tube and connected it to a needle in the back of the viney vein on the back of my hand.

A few hours later I felt like I was a blacktop driveway, covered with snow. First the snowplow would come, then the sun would heat the driveway, then the snow would blow back, and the plow would come back over it again.

For three days I vomited. The nurse from the cancer center in Philadelphia called to find out how I was doing. She told Tom I could get a prescription that would help. He explained they had already given me a drug for that at the time I had the chemo treatment. I had Xanax in the I.V. But the nurse told him I was supposed to be taking something else as well. The nurse told him to call Dr. Apple. So he did. Dr. Apple said, "Yes, we have something for that. If it is needed." Tom said it was. About ten minutes later Tom came home with the new prescription. The medicine worked. By Monday, only five days into this chemotherapy I could get up and do normal human things again. I believed I could get through this.

We celebrated Mariah's seventeenth birthday. Mariah was truly a young woman, with her own dreams and her own life. Only a year and a few months from graduation from high school she had begun planning for college. Her grandparents gave her a set of luggage for her birthday to symbolize her impending independence. In just a year she would be old enough to be on her own if "something were to happen to us" as they say.

The Seed Catalogue Came

Even when no else believes in Spring, the seed companies send out catalogues with page after page of beautiful flowers and fruits and vegetables.

I thought about the bare earth outside under the hard coating of frost. I wondered if I would ever be able to turn the soil, and plant my usual token vegetable garden. I pictured myself in July, bald and frail standing over these clods of barren clay, wishing for an organic carrot, or a fresh piece of broccoli. The thought of not planting a garden this year seemed a most horrific affront this illness could possibly serve.

Does cancer mean I can't smell the springtime earth, or see the new sprouts of beans and squash standing boldly in their little rows? Will I have no flowers to define the season, or harvest of tomatoes and egg plants to create those healthy meals my family politely accepts just because it is August?

Gardening was not part of my suburban upbringing. This gardening thing came first as a possible way to get food, when Tom was a seminary student, and my little paychecks were our only source of income. Money was scarce. We had a chance to use a section of a community garden plot at the seminary apartments. I picked up a stack of free "how-to" flyers published by the seed companies. I read about how to plan, dig, plant, fertilize, kill bugs, weed and harvest. The pamphlets were written with the idea that the reader had actually seen a garden. So I was totally surprised to find out some of the most obvious things that the written words had omitted.

We liked tomatoes. So I read that each tomato plant needs about 3 feet of space around it, and a stake to support it. I read that it is better for a beginner to buy tomato plants already started. It did not say what tomato plants looked like, or how big they got, or where the tomatoes would appear on the branches. When I got to the nursery I was surprised to see how tiny and frail the tomato plants looked. I tried to imagine a large tomato sitting atop of this tiny twig. I knew we could use two dozen tomatoes, and I was sure that some of those tiny little stems would not support the heavy fruit, so I bought extras. I put out thirty tomato plants, exactly according to the directions in the books. I wanted two dozen tomatoes.

I spent many hours that year, weeding, watering, and watching the plants and the seeds grow. Of course I had heard about the idea of abundance. The familiar Thanksgiving hymn tells about it, "first the blade and then the ear, then the full corn shall appear."[9] But I had no idea this was so profound a miracle waiting to be found among the simple facts of nature. The thirty tiny tomato sprouts that I hardly believed could survive each grew as tall as I am, and the tiny stakes I put out were a comical understatement. We harvested two dozen tomatoes — from each plant. I had sixty times my highest hope. The next year I only planted six tomato plants, and when we had plenty of tomatoes. I was not surprised.

That is how it is with so many pieces of God's magnificent Creation. At first I am in awe. The gifts are more than I could have ever wished. Then I begin to accept it, and then to expect it. I keep on growing tomatoes as a reminder that what may seem like a routine chore to the accomplished gardener, is really a miraculous gift.

Now as I deal with this life threatening disease, the tomato lesson is important. Life itself is one of those miraculous gifts larger, and more beautiful than we could have ever wished. And in our little human struggle to define what is bigger than we are, people calculate a "life expectancy" — 72 years is a current average number for women. So, if we get less years we are disappointed. If we have more years we beat the odds and "win." But in reality, the gift of life is not measured in years. It is found in the days, and seconds, the moments of beauty. The quantity of years we call "life expectancy" is not really what we expect from life at all. Just as six tomato plants fill my need for tomatoes, my life does not have to have 72 years for me to feel it is of great value.

I flipped through the pages of the seed catalogue, and began to fill in the order form. Maybe I would not be able to

---

[9]A line from the hymn "Come Ye Thankful People Come" by Henry Alford, 1894.

plant a garden this year. But February is not the time to give up that plan.

The doctors were strictly opposed to my being out in the sun. Both chemotherapy and radiation are adversely affected by sunlight. So I ordered a large brimmed garden hat, when I placed the seed order.

Letters

Each day I felt fine. In fact, I was actually feeling more energetic, and less pain than I had in many months. They say you have no pain with breast cancer, but now that it was gone, I had relief from pain, so there must have been something to feel.

I had lots of cards to answer. I heard from well over one hundred people from the churches that Tom had served, as well as family and friends. But the odd thing was that people who write letters to healthy people are an altogether different group of people than the people who write to cancer patients. The personal identity dimension of the disease was raising its irrational ugly head again. It was like I had a special new halo around me, and some people thought it was magic, and others avoided it like, shall I say, like the plague. Other cancer patients wrote to me. We seemed to share a sisterhood of suffering. People I had not heard from in years suddenly answered ancient Christmas cards with personal telephone calls.

Jan, a friend who was a pastor in a rural Ohio church was the one person I knew who had chemo therapy for breast cancer, and was still alive. Jan answered my letter with a couple of pages welcoming me to the "sisterhood" so to speak. I received the letter before I started on the series of chemo treatments. Jan's letter was kind but straight forward. She had told of her experience. At the time I thought her letter was a horrific initiation rite to a sorority I never chose. When I got the letter I hid it in the back of my journal, and tried to convince myself I hadn't opened it. But in the back of my mind, I knew what it said. She talked about losing her hair, and wearing a wig. She said she had a bad week after treatments, but she had her treatments early in the week, and she was able to continue her preaching schedule.

After my first treatment I read the letter again. This time it was not the least bit scarey. The same words were comforting, and filled with encouragement. It's sort of the Ecclesiastics Effect. When times are tough it is assuring to know that change is imminent. When you are looking up from the bottom of a well the little opening of light at the top is always light, even at midnight, in a rain storm. There is a time to worry about chemo therapy, and a time to wallow in the new found freedom from the fear of it.

As I looked through the stack of well wishes, I could hear people struggling for the right words as I always do when I write to someone who is dealing with something I don't even want to think about. I learned that there are no wrong words. Any words are good words. The only empty, hurt feelings I had were when people with whom I had been corresponding, did not write at all.

I was that person. When I was starting out on my own, just out of college, in my early twenties, I shared an apartment in Rockland, Maine with a roommate, Kathy. She had a zest for the adventurous life for which I also yearned, and she actually accomplished it. She was always coming back from big weekends skiing, or traveling to exotic places. Kathy had been diagnosed with epilepsy which caused her to stumble every time she went up stairs. We joked about the routine way she always tripped on exactly the same stair. She took medicine for it, so she never had seizures, but she often had immobilizing headaches.

On one of our Sunday morning adventures we went out to a large lake where a race track had been plowed in the deep snow. In that time and place a favorite winter sport was racing cars on ice. And this was a day for a big race. The track was several miles long by the time it circled the whole lake. It was several traffic lanes wide, and had steep snow banks on both sides. Kathy and I decided to ice skate the track. We skated and skated for a good hour, and we were probably half way around the lake, when Kathy stumbled. She said she was very tired, and her head was pounding. We sat down to rest. Then we realized we had only an hour left before the cars would be arriving, and we had to get off the track. We had only our ice skates, and crossing the snow would be hard to do even if we had snow shoes, so we just continued skating. Most of the way, I pulled her along, as she was clearly too tired to skate very much. A few times she fell, but each time she got up to go again, I could see this was probably our stupidest adventure. We made it back to our car and our shoes. But her headaches never subsided. She went back to her parent's home to get her "head examined" as we joked.

I was watching an ad for a skin cream to treat, "the heartbreak of psoriasis" when the phone call came from Kathy's mother confirming that Kathy had a brain tumor, and she had to have emergency surgery that day to relieve pressure and that surgery had left her paralyzed. The tumor was malignant, and they were unable to remove it. To this day I think the skin cream company exaggerated the seriousness of psoriasis.

I know her mother could not understand my fear of medical things at the time. So I tried to visit Kathy in the hospital. Each time I started to go from the waiting room of the hospital into the hall toward her room I could feel that stainless steel in my veins, and I knew I had to sit down, and get my breath before trying again. Finally I got down the hall to her room. I carried a paper cup of water hoping it would help me stay conscious. There was Kathy, head all bandaged, just as bound up in medical paraphernalia as I had feared, but she was smiling her usual warm smile, and I knew she understood that I was glad to see her, but that I could not deal with the medical stuff. (She knew about my fear.) I left and passed out in the elevator. But it was so good to see her again.

I tried to write to her, but I couldn't think of what to say. Everything sounded like the "heartbreak of psoriasis," in perspective. I heard from her mother that Kathy and her long time boyfriend had a chance to travel to India before she died. I know she had a chance to say good bye to the world and the life that she loved. But I needed to say good-bye to her.

CHAPTER 3

Hair Today, Goon Tomorrow

"Little bunny Foo Foo
Hoppin' through the forest
Pickin' up field mice and
Poppen 'em on the head."[10]

nd the children's verse goes on in dialogue format with the voice of the disciplinarian/ narrator finally declaring Foo Foo a "goon." It's easy to know what Bunny Foo Foo did to get that title. He picked up field mice, and popped them on the head. The whole story is about justice, which luckily, I don't believe in. If I did believe in justice I would be a victim of injustice. And I don't really feel like a victim.

One day, a week or two after my first treatment, my clothes, the carpet, everything took a strange metallic silver look. Then I realized, that was my hair. I knew this was coming, so I had already looked up "hair" in the yellow pages, and I had found a place that makes wigs especially for cancer patients. I knew it was time to go there.

We found that this "wig place," does not sell "wigs" at all. They have "hair systems" or "cranial prostheses." A hair system looks like a wig, and feels like a wig and quacks like a wig.

---

[10]"Little Bunny Foo Foo" is a traditional children's finger game.

I was ready to say to Antonio, the trained hair system specialist, "go ahead and cut all this falling hair off now. Let me be bald, not just shaggy". But Tom was reluctant . He did not want to make any "snap decisions" about something this important. I knew we did not have a choice of when or if I lose my hair. We could only decide where the hair would fall. But I could see that Tom needed a little more time to make this adjustment. So, we thought about it for twenty-four hours. It felt much more like it was a choice we had made when we went back the next day. The "hair system specialist" shaved the hair I had left so that it was about ½ inch long. But those patches of hair only lasted another day, then I was completely shiny, skin only, bald, just like any stereotypical space alien. For the first time in my life I could see what my head looked like. I even had hair in my baby picture, so this was something completely new to me.

For a secret clown this was a fine time — hats, wigs, flowers — lots of options, lots of characters to play. I actually had a clown character. Before cancer made me really bald, as a clown I covered my serious hair with a white balding pate wig with bright red yarn fringe hair.

Pidgy, my clown character is derived from a character I imagine being a seller of sacrificial pigeons at the Jerusalem Temple on the day when Jesus visited and became angered at the mercenary emphasis in the holy place. Jesus tipped over the tables of the money changers. That caused a big mess because the coins that had been sorted by country were now a homogenous mix. The pilgrims who came from far off lands had to change their coinage to fit the national order of Jerusalem. When Jesus came along and made this mess, it was clear that one coin was not much different from the next. It made kind of a symbolic, everyone is valuable statement. Then, Jesus let go the pigeons which were blessed for sacrifice. I imagine the pigeon seller, Pidgy, running around frantically bemoaning the fact that you can't tell the holy little peckers from the common park pigeons! That's what Jesus did, and does. Jesus as the manifestation of God, takes what human beings designate as special and holy, and makes it seem common. Or is it that mixing the holy with the profane and seeing no difference is the awakening that we are all holy? The common park pigeons are holy. The little bald priest who was selling pigeons as especially blessed, he is holy too. Oh, he wants people to think he is holy. He is a pompous little priest. But in the broader scope of things, he really is holy, and he is the one who has a hard time believing it. That's who Pidgy is, and that's why I like to step inside that clown character from time to time, and see how the world looks from this point of the profane.

As a clown I had learned a lesson about people. Appearance is everything. When I went out into the world as a clown version of an assertive bald priest, instead of my usual short, childlike female, people took me more seriously even though I was a clown. Pidgy the clown had cartoon features painted on for a face, and yarn for hair, and yet he gets a more dignified reception in public than do I.

So, as I entered my middle years, and my hair started to accumulate a few gray hairs, I rejoiced and let it do its thing. As a gray haired women my youthfulness was not an issue. People started to view me as an adult. Store clerks waited on me. People in line recognized that I was filling the spot in front of them not just hanging around with someone who was in line. I got a more professional job. My silver crown gave me a kind of royalty I had never experienced as a youthful looking short woman.

Now this hairlessness offered me a choice of "hair" colors and styles. I tried on my old color, of dark brown. I looked like a kid again, but a really ugly, short kid. So my wig choice was silver, with dark hair around the edges, just like my long gone real hair. But being a reasonably priced wig, it was much shorter than my old hair.

My first appearance at church in the wig brought many compliments. People thought I had a hair cut. I was not at all prepared for people not to have any idea I was wearing a wig, and then to think I looked better. Its quite a twist to have what I assumed to be total devastation of my appearance to end up an improvement.

I soon found that a hat with a wig is awkward, because they both come off at the same time, especially when one's head is the texture of a light bulb. So, when I went someplace where I wore a coat most of the time, like to the store, I wore a hat, and no gray locks. I found I was right back to the old "short kid" image again. Clerks would count my coins carefully, assuming my arithmetic skills may not have been fully developed. Nobody asked, "May I help you, Ma'am." "See where that girl is standing." I heard the store clerk say. Just when I was beginning to accept the fact that I was a woman in my fifties I had to deal with the indignities of being a teen. It must be very hard to really be a kid.

Now, driving is a whole different story. My old gray curls must have been saying to cars behind me "The car ahead of you will go to slow, so pass it as quick as you can, at all costs." While a baseball hat says, "This is no old lady. It must be a normal driver. You can stay in your own lane and drive behind this car." I guess the next step to gaining an authoritative image behind the wheel is to wear my wide brimmed garden hat when I drive. If I place it straight on my head, my silhouette will be that of a Boy Scout, or maybe a Highway Patrol officer. Now there's a plan.

At times I missed my hair. My hair had been really nice hair. The hair system specialist cut it and wrapped it so I could save it. He said he could make a hair fringe with it, for me to wear with hats. So, even though we could never afford the professionally hand made fringe, it seemed practical to save the hair, and it helped with the grief process of losing it. I did take it out and look at it from time to time. The promise was the hair grows back, only most people find it is different, and a lot of cancer patients say they like it better.

Having no hair, and a developing self concept as a "cancer patient" testing even normal looking hair and hats was something of a struggle. So I did not venture as far into the creative as I might have done.

A Will is a Plan the Planner Won't See

Tom and I visited the lawyer to prepare our wills. Despite the pessimism implied in writing a will, Tom and I found that our unspoken fears for Mariah's future would be banished by confronting them, and preparing for the worst. What if I were to die of cancer, and Mariah would have only one parent and lots of grief? What if we were both gone? The narrow line between life and death is crossed as easily squishing a cabbage worm on the great green leaf on which it feasted. And I would at least be as caring a parent as the cabbage worm butterfly who chooses a safer place to lay her eggs, once she sees the gardener is squishing caterpillars. So it seemed very important that we create a plan for Mariah that would see her through a hard time. We wanted to know she would have people who would care about her future.

Both of our brothers were single then, and their life styles did not include teens. Tom's parents were in a retirement community -- not really an appropriate place for a young woman to live, not to mention the imposition on them. My parents were so busy trying to fit thousands of years of living into their "golden years," I think Mariah's hopes for college would be put aside so they could pursue their activities. We thought about our friends who were couples. We thought of Sara and Phil Morgan.

When Mariah was barely three years old we started her in dance and music because she was intensively involved in reading, which she picked up on her own, at this early age. We wanted her to develop in all areas. She needed things to interest her in physical activities to develop her motor skills, and also, we felt it was important for her to have a social environment with others her own age. In our rural Ohio town we found a dancing school, but we had to drive to a nearby city with a university, to find a music program for three and four year olds. Along with dance, we enrolled her in a Suzuki violin program.

She really enjoyed listening to the music, and the games and repetitions that made the lessons appropriate for this young child. Then we moved to a suburban area near Dayton, Ohio, when Mariah was starting to kindergarten.

I tried every lead I could to find a new Suzuki teacher. One possibility was an older woman who had been a traditional teacher many years but decided she did not like working with teenagers, so she read a book on the Japanese methods of teaching young children, and now she was ready to try it. We all tried. But it was apparent that the pairing of this teacher and Mariah was inappropriate. She kept saying that she did not know that a five year old could act so much like a teenager, "and with her mother right there watching!" I was watching, and I could see she did not enjoy Mariah's five year old wit, and didactic learning style. I think she thought young children were blank cassette tapes on which she could record her lessons. Questions like, "Why do I need to practice when I can already play it?" were construed as "talking back."

We then found another Suzuki teacher in the area, who had an excellent reputation. But she would not take Mariah because Mariah's first teacher had not put enough emphasis on posture, and Mariah would have to start the whole curriculum over again. She felt five years old was too old to start over.

We found a high school girl who had just started taking violin in the school orchestra, and was at the same level as Mariah. We hired her as a practice partner. Mariah looked forward to her visits, and thrived on sharing her interest in music with someone, but as the months went on the high school girl apparently lost interest in the violin, and gave up practicing and stopped coming over.

I saw this little child trying to step into this huge new world we had moved to with an all new school, and new church, with all new expectations of her, and no one who cared at all about her interest in music. Her violin became relegated to a show and tell oddity. I wished we could find just one person who liked both children, and music. I prayed for just one little favor from God. I said, "Dear God, I am not asking for a real miracle, you don't have to send an angel, or any special heavenly envoy, we just want to be introduced to one person who loves children and who plays the violin who could be a part of this little child's life this year, when she needs this. If you send us the name of this person I will make the phone call, and do all the driving." I did not ask for an angel, but somehow I knew that God would send nothing less.

A few days later a neighbor brought an ad she had clipped from the newspaper. "I saw this picture of a little girl playing the violin, and I thought of Mariah." It pictured a small child with a violin, and under the picture was an advertisement for the Suzuki Method for teaching violin. The lessons were being offered in a renovated school building only one block from our new house. I called for an appointment, and a day later Mariah and I walked over to the neighborhood art center to meet this new teacher.

There, in a little room surrounded by children's art work and small colorful chairs, was a smiling young woman, with a violin. She looked for all the world like something that should be on the top of a Christmas tree. It only took a few

minutes to know that this smiling woman, Miss Ritchie, had a fabulous gift for combining children with music.

She had just received her masters degree in teaching Suzuki Violin, and she had recently moved to Dayton to near her fiancé, Phil, and to begin her career teaching violin. Sara started a very popular program, so as the years passed, there were other children Mariah's age, who came for group lessons, and parties, and playing the violin did not seem at all strange and unusual.

Now, all these years later, Mariah has also become a beautiful violinist who also loves children. Phil and Sara are dear friends of ours. And I have not stopped saying "Thank you God, for sending these beautiful people into our lives."

We thought of Phil and Sara when we had to imagine Mariah without us. If our will named them, they would allow Mariah to fulfill her dreams of going to college, and they would allow her to seek the spiritual support she would need to get through a time of loss. We called them, and they agreed to be her guardians if they were needed before she turned eighteen, in a year.

March, 97

Second Treatment and Entirely Too Much Television

I was less apprehensive before the second treatment. I knew that the mysterious colored liquids pouring into my veins would most definitely make me sick. There was no reason to expect anything else. And that was all there was to it. Just before my second treatment Dr. Apple talked with me about the side effects that I had experienced with the first treatment. I mentioned that my elbows and knees hurt, and they had distinct red marks on them.   I was sure the Adrimycin, that gaudy, bright coral colored stuff, was leaking out of my veins at the joints, and that is what appeared on my skin. It was sort of a bean bag toy idea. If you pour beans or stuffing in, and there is a worn spot the beans will spill out. Dr. Apple didn't buy that theory. He thought it might be an allergy, and I was supposed to report on it if it happened again.

Laura had a little trouble finding the vein in my hand, and I was aware that one of the side effects of this chemo is weaker veins. During the hour I spent with Laura while she was putting the chemicals into my veins, I asked about the possibility of getting a "medi-port." That is a little device, surgically mounted under the skin, which accesses the vena cava. Of all the grotesque, scarey things I could imagine, this one is at the top of my list of personal worsts. It was as if the Gingerbread Man was asking to be baked with teeth marks. She suggested I gather information from others who had it, and from the surgeon. In the weeks to come I followed her suggestion.

Laura pulled out the tubes, and the second treatment was done, and I had only to await the side effects.

I knew what to expect from chemo, and also I knew what to expect from another marathon of daytime television. After a very short time I found the Cathode Ray Tube distraction totally predictable. Daytime T.V. is a window on the world for sick people. There are contests where everyone is hyper, and the slowest thinker, often wins huge amounts of money. They win prizes like "Recreational Vehicles" (Does that mean that cars without kitchens are not recreational?) And they win cruises to some hot place, that isn't Hell.

Flip through the stations and catch a talk show, when a panel of sick, large sized people who used to be at home watching television, actually show up in person to do mean things to one another. They cry about things they felt they deserved, and retribution is the accepted standard of justice.

Then there are the "soaps." which aren't really sponsored by soap at all anymore, but by health insurance companies, by hospitals, and by drug companies. These show the lives of the sick and the hopeless played by actors who are sick and restless, or perhaps, young and hopeless. All of this programming tends to suck the energy out of a healthy person, but if you are sick, it is your whole world in a box.

So, I spent three days throwing up, and changing channels. Finally Saturday came, and I thought, this is the new day for which I have been waiting. Today, PBS would have adult programming all day long. I could watch people building houses, doing crafts, fixing things, growing gardens, backpacking through Europe. This is the day I can get well again. But un-be-knownst to me, this was one of those special weeks when PBS changes its format to let the public pledge their support.

This Saturday morning included a beautifully prepared show combining nature and music. That would have been perfect, except that it was an hour of hot air balloon photography, dipping into foaming waterfalls, while an extra loud medley of "Swan Lake" and "Night on Bald Mountain" offered non-stop sound.

I think if that didn't make healthy people nauseous the two hour balloon trip over Pennsylvania that offered a local tour of nature could do it. The sound track for this was all the instruments of the orchestra produced electronically on a single, over-dubbed, synthesizer, which I assume was being played in the balloon basket, by the soft voiced woman who was narrating our tour. It was all swaying back and forth at the same pitch as the balloon. After three hours of this, the station offered the opportunity to call in and have this whole series of tapes sent directly to your house.

I actually was longing to see the beautiful Pennsylvania countryside, but I really wanted to see it from a stationary window that week.

There is a parallel to chemotherapy and mountain climbing. Both involve days of organizing and preparing, then comes the journey, the physical fatigue, the long haul, the

blisters in odd places, itches, chills, all the annoyances with no actual pain... some close camaraderie and some obnoxious people too, and always the long haul that only your own body can do. The important thing is always to look out over the valleys, and keep the complete perspective. There is a great value in being able to focus on the goal, and to continue to go in that direction. The harder the climb, the more beautiful is the respite at the top.

I went back to Dr. Finn, and got the flyer about medi-ports. He talked with me about the surgery, but he did not have an actual medi-port to show me. I feared it might be made of stainless steel. The brochure showed some plastic and some stainless steel models. I asked him as the surgery was scheduled to try hard to avoid those stainless steel ones. I'm sure he didn't listen. No one would tell me what kind it was, and when they put it in, my face was covered with that blue cloth thing they use in the operating room.

April, 1997

A Port In Any Storm

Television news programs reported on the mass suicides of the "Heaven's Gate" cult as I was preparing the Easter Sunday School lesson for my sixth grade class. According to reports thirty-nine bright young and middle aged web site designers were followers of a leader who reportedly claimed that Heaven's Gate was to be found by taking a space ship which was following the comet Hale-Bopp. The news media reported that it was thought that in order to gain passage on this space ship these cult members were led to believe that one must die. So, according to the various news reports, these thirty-nine people very methodically, wearing matching clothes, and tennis shoes, took poison, laid down on their beds to die, and were covered, each with a purple cloth.

I thought of the sixth graders in my Sunday School class. They were for the most part, bright, computer literate, and they were searching for real answers to questions like: Where is heaven? So I wrote this letter to my class:

Dear Class,

A few weeks ago Jenny asked "so where is heaven? We've been in space and it's not there."

When Jenny asked this important question I asked her to read "The Kingdom of Heaven" parables throughout the Gospel of Matthew (There are parallels in Mark and Luke as well.) Jesus used simple earthly symbols to talk about what we do not see with our scientific five senses. Jesus said, the Kingdom of Heaven is like an experience of wanting a pearl or the growing of a mustard seed or yeast, or a person who finds a treasure.

Here is what I know. Before there was space or earth or people, there was God, and as some of us talk of God, there was a Creator, a Christ, a Holy Spirit. Our spiritual life is real now, and it is heaven. But it is not something we can always touch, or see, or smell or taste or hear.

The world that we know with our physical senses is beautiful. It is the world of our bodies, our music, flowers, stars, space, earth, meteors, comets, other people. Its beauty opens a tiny peephole into heaven, as a love song opens a tiny window on what love is. The tangible world was created by God and by its very definition in creation it is 'good' but it is not all there is. Our spiritual lives are already part of our living. Some people feel an awareness of the spiritual now. Other's expect death will sharpen their awareness and that they will become more spiritual after death. Is one way right? How would anyone know? God only knows.

The next week after we talked about the 'Kingdom of Heaven' as the Gospels of Mark and Matthew use that phrase, I was out one evening and saw a comet in the sky. It was very spectacular--with a blue light trailing in the tail and the head moving around like a living thing. I know you are a smart group of sixth graders. So, that Sunday I asked you, 'Does anyone know about a comet in the sky?' And sure enough a flood of information poured out. Christie even knew when and who had first discovered it. It is 'Hale-Bopp.'

You are indeed a smart class— good in science, kind to one another, sensitive, you have got it all. But also, they say, the people of the 'Heaven's Gate Cult' were all of those good things. And that concerns me. I am afraid for you in this strange world where cyberspace seems real, and reality is more confused by good clear thinking.

I am afraid that when you find yourselves in a time of loneliness, or lostness, you will lose sight of God's grace.

Things that you find that look like a pathway to heaven will be appealing to you, just because you are bright and sensitive. How will you know what is really God's way of guiding you to heaven's gate?

Let me share with you some of my personal experiences lately to help shed light on the use of suicide, as a means to a faith journey.

If you saw me without my wig you would think I was trying to look like some mystical monk, or member of a cult. I am completely bald. I have no hair.

On the morning of that same day that the people in the Heaven's Gate cult were lying down on their narrow beds, covering their faces with a cloth, taking the suicide drugs, I too was lying on a narrow bed, while drugs were poured into my veins, and to separate me from reality my face was covered with blue cloth. I was in the operating room having surgery to receive a special device implanted under my skin, so that chemicals which have already poisoned my veins and taken my hair could more easily be pumped into my body.

For me, since I believe that the "Kingdom of Heaven" is real, and that life exists beyond death, death is not scary. What is frightening is people who know only physical things, taking control of my mind and body, separating me from my prayers. So why did I let myself get into this situation where doctors and drugs control my body?

A few months ago, I found that I had a tumor which is cancer. Right where my heart should have been beating was this strange new growth like a comet from space — no reason for it— confusing to scientists — sort of amazing — but definitely physically real.

My first thought was, since I am not afraid of death because of my faith in God who is a spiritual reality, and I am afraid of doctors, operations and drugs, why not just die?

Then I realized that I love my husband, my daughter, my parents — I care about you — I haven't even heard your questions about God — I don't even know you very well yet. I want more time with you.

God gave me things on earth that I love: trees and animals, beautiful scenery, music, friends, family, all these physical things are little lovely symbols of God's heavenly beauty. Physical things may not be all there is to life, but they are valuable gifts from God. Just as we respect a cross or a flag because they are symbols, so too should we respect our physical bodies. They are a symbol of the spiritual life. I knew that, and with the help of people whom I love I decided that I should choose life over death, even though I am afraid of something ugly like a tumor, and of the medical procedures used to take the tumor away.

I decided to give healing science a try. The surgery has left some scars on my body. In the name of healing I have had chemicals poured into my blood taking my hair, my veins, and my strength. I have yet to face radiation treatment. But also I know I have found loving, caring people in this physical life that I would have missed knowing had I simply died from the tumor. So what's the difference between me, either living or dying with cancer and these thirty-nine people either living or dying when they follow Hale-Bopp?

Do you remember the story about the Golden Calf that the Isrealites made because they thought God had abandoned them in the dessert? It was an idol. It was a physical symbol that had become more important than a heavenly reality. The physical statue replaced God. A cross or a church can become an idol if that physical thing becomes worshiped more than the spiritual God. Our physical bodies can be idols if we worship them and forget our spiritual life. A physical heaven in the sky or a comet, or a UFO can be a physical idol replacing the spiritual God if we worship it. Worshiping these things, instead of using them for symbols or tools of understanding spiritual life is what idolatry is.

The all-loving God, creator of physical symbols of life does not ask for our physical death. When death comes to us, God carries us through it and keeps our spiritual lives safe. It is idolatry that kills people for religious reasons. People killed

Jesus because they confused the physical symbol, Jesus's body, with the heavenly life.

Easter is a day of pagan symbols being broken opened and shattered so that the life can be seen and God can be the only thing we worship. My wish for you is that you value and cherish God's symbols and gifts: physical life, love, music, art, your bodies, your scientific knowledge, the wonders of sky and earth, living things, other worlds, — please know, love, and cherish all these things, but don't worship anything but God. Worship God, only, and you will be safe from these suicide cults. All the stuff you see, touch, taste, smell, hear is just stuff, good stuff, a lot of it is, but it is just stuff. What you know with your heart, your prayers, your experiences with God, that is what is real and loving."

On Easter we had a busy morning. The hour was too short for my sermonizing, so this was what I really had time to say:

"Thank you God, for life, and love.

Guide us in your way.

Let us know that we are the loving work of your fingers on earth and our lives are of great value."

Half - Way

The last struggle to find my veins in my hand before surgery had left my whole hand and arm full of bruises. These bruises were a badge affirming the choice to get the Mediport. So one week after that surgery I handed my flesh and bones back to the Medical Oncology Unit to continue the great experiment in healing.

This Third treatment took the form of the basic Seventh Grade Science project. It was an experiment to show the cause of the rash. After the second treatment, the little red lines at my knees and elbows had become a widespread raised rash. Dr. Apple decided to experiment to find which of the drugs was causing this, he eliminated one of the three drugs and see if the rash returned. Like a wayward white mouse, I mentioned that it could also be the Xanax, the fourth drug given for nausea. So he eliminated that one as well, leaving me with only the bright coral Adrymycin, and the Cytoxen.

A few hours later I had a much greater appreciation for the Xanax, and also I could see the rash returning. That meant I would have to go back to the hospital to get the drug that was left out, the 5 Flourouraal. This experiment had narrowed the rash cause down to either the Cytoxen or the Adrymycin.

The next day I was reduced to a barfing bag of bones with a hat. Tom took me back to the hospital on his lunch break. The oncologist on call was Dr. Sorroco. She was the tall, dark haired woman who bothers to read the manuals. She was quite concerned about the "rash" now called "severe allergic reaction." But also, she seemed concerned about me She did not think my odd shaped breast was every woman's dream of youthfulness. She did not talk about the "ladies" she has treated. She talked to me, even though Tom was in the room.

I did get the chemo drug, and the Xanax and a steroid for the "severe allergic reaction." And I got the promise that the next treatment will be another phase of this science project. Another drug will be taken out of the mix, to see if I, this white mouse am still allergic. Personally I would prefer the role of the Seventh Grader in this science project.

Which reminded me of cats. I had exactly the same kind of allergy to cats as I had to the chemo therapy. I asked Dr. Apple if there was a similarity to any of the drugs in question to cat dander. He said, "We don't make medicine out of cats." Which only made me wonder out of what do they make this stuff?

And I have always thought that the cat allergy was more heart and mind than actual physical affliction, even though it clearly had physical consequences. That was because of my childhood relationship with the cat Dusty Tom, before I had an allergy to cats.

I first met Dusty at my Grandparent's farm. When we visited Grandpa and Grandma Heitzman on the farm Jack and I always scrambled to get a look at the evening milking ritual. (The morning milking was a little too early for us city-folk.) But in the evening when we heard Grandpa rattling pails in the milk house we knew it was time to go outside and down the lane, where Bootsie the dog was heading to the cow pasture. Somehow Grandpa and Grandma's fuzzy old house pet knew this chore. He went about it with amazing expertise. Bootsie went ahead of Grandpa out to the pasture. He squeezed under the lowest rung of the gate, so that by the time Grandpa got to the gate to open it, Bootsie already had the cows standing in a single file line on the little mud path leading up to the barn. Grandpa would swing the gate opened. He would say two of his rare words, "Hea Boots." Then the tidy procession would go through the gate, cross the road, and, with Bootsie still nipping at the heels of the last bovine, they would go into the barnyard area. Then, one by one they would be brought into the stall for a turn to be milked. Grandpa knew the personality of each cow. We children could go close to some, and we could even go into the stall with others. While there were some cows we were not allowed near, and we had to be very quiet during the milking of those. Among living creatures on the farm, grandchildren are the most useless. On a farm being human doesn't seem to put one at an advantage as it does in other settings.

The last cow to be milked was usually the most gentle of all of Grandpa's milk cows. The cats were waiting in the loft and they knew it was their turn, so they moved in closer too. Grandpa put aside his pail of milk, and allowed Jack and me each a turn to come into the stall, and sit on the little stool, and milk the cow. We were to fill a pie pan for the new kittens, who were just being weaned. Grandpa brought in an armful of tiny kittens. There was Dusty Tom. He was a tiny, soft blue-gray ball of fluff, like something from the lint trap in the dryer, until I got a look at his face. He had that wise, and independent look that is so peculiar to cats. He seemed to know everything before his life, and everything after. He had the wisdom of all times and places, and he was only six weeks old. I took him into the house. That night he slept in a box by my bed. And from then on, he was my cat.

Recently I heard cat owners being asked if they believed their cats would save their lives if they were in danger. I giggle at the picture this conjures in my mind's eye. It seems many cat owners do believe their cats would save their lives. That is so funny to me now. But I can assure you, when Dusty was alive, I would have been first in line to offer Dusty Tom as the quintessential rescue cat.

One Christmas season our family went away for the day Christmas shopping in the city. We were gone a very long time, and we knew we had left Dusty locked up in the house longer than he had ever been before. Dusty was an indoor/outdoor kind of cat, so we never had an inside litter box for him. When we returned we could tell by the odor in the living room that Dusty had not waited for us to let him out. But we could not find any cat poop to clean up, so we could not pay proper penance for our tardiness, and also, we couldn't solve the smell problem. As the hours wore on, it became an intensive search, somehow focused on the odoriferous area surrounding the Christmas tree which was filled with wrapped gifts. We moved the gifts out carefully whiffing each parcel, still no sign of a cat mess.

Dusty, in the meantime, was pacing around nervously beside himself with guilt. Nothing we could say or do seemed to relieve his anxiety over breaking the cardinal rule of housecatness.

Finally, with all the gifts carefully removed and inspected, the odor still came from the base of the tree. That's when we found it. Dusty had neatly and precisely filled the tiny little water cup which surrounded the trunk to the tree— the tree being the only sign of outdoors he could identify.

Then came the task of removing the tree from the house. Somehow that process happened while Jack and I slept, with all the stealth of a visit from Santa. We celebrated Christmas that year around a beautiful drawing of a tree that

Mom had created for the occasion. It neither smelled like pine nor cat poop.

Dusty Tom lived life as my pet for about seven years. He died of some cat disease the veterinarian was powerless to cure. Then, for the first time in my life I had felt a deep loss.

Mom and Dad tried to help in the healing by taking me back to Grandpa's and Grandma's farm just when a new litter of kittens was ready to be weaned. The tiny kittens were adorable. But of course, none had that timeless look of wisdom that made Dusty Tom so unique. Even the blue gray tom cat was not the same. I petted the gray kitten, and I put it back in the box. That was when I first discovered I was allergic to cats. Every part of my skin that had touched the cat was swelling and itchy. My eyes were watering. I could hardly breathe. All up and down my arm I had welts shaped like cat paws. We have had pet dogs ever since. And until I tried chemotherapy, cats were the only thing to which I have ever been allergic. I have always believed that I had that reaction to cats because of my loss of Dusty Tom. For a long time I believed it was totally psychosomatic because the allergy is decidedly worse when the cat fur was gray, like Dusty's.

Then, a few years ago I was in a play where I wore a gray fake fur coat. After each rehearsal my skin would get swollen and itchy wherever the coat touched me. The label in the coat assured me it was completely 100 % synthetic, and I believed it was impossible for this allergy to be a physical thing, so I tried every method I could to make myself think the coat was not a gray cat. Finally I talked to the director, who had also donated the coat to the costume department, and I tried to arrange to wear something less like my old cat Dusty. She apologized, and explained that I am not the only one who thinks the coat is like a gray cat. Her own Russian Blue cat had made that old coat his home. In that case, dry cleaning the coat ended my allergic reaction. And I accepted the fact that cat dander is possibly physical not just psychological.

All Purpose Hopes and Fears to Hold Onto All the Years

The common good advice people gave me was "have hope you will be healed." I tried to get a handle on hope. And finally I gave up. Well, I didn't give up believing in healing, I simply gave up calling it "hope."

Hope is almost as overrated as a virtuous perspective as justice is. They sound great! Who wouldn't want justice? Who wouldn't want hope? But when you really get down to the nitty-gritty of life, hope and justice are simply words to fill up an empty space where a void is still a void. Justice is the great excuse for "getting even." It causes wars, and negates forgiveness. It is used by "good people" as a reason to ignore the teachings in the Gospels. And hope is just as counter-productive. Hope is the lie that says "I have a positive attitude, anyway despite the fact that I can see only the negative." It is the word that really defines giving up. "We can always hope," is another way of saying " there is no chance in Hell." Hope gets in the way of useful concepts like dealing with ugly truths straight on, and like believing in God's power beyond our understanding — believing in miracles. Hope is a word the Gospels avoid, but the book of Job relishes.

"I hope, you hope, we hope," it is so easy to say, and yet to believe in hopelessness. "Hope" has become a euphemism for "just pretend not to give up." We forget that "hope" could mean "assurance" or "expectation." In conversations with doctors it is easy to get them to say "we always hope." But they never say, "we can always assure." We can't really ask doctors for more than hope. They are only human. But in conversations with God we can ask for assurance. Hope is not what keeps us going. Assurance is.

I figure if you can't call it a plan or an intention you can't call it anything. So, on my way to give up on hoping and start believing I turned my reading to plans to find a cure for cancer. I learned that the treatment I was having was the same old standby that had failed my cousin Gwen ten years earlier. It was the same routine they had been putting people through for the last twenty years. Some new advances had been made in radiation, but the chemo I was getting was the same old stuff that may or may not work. Who knows?

In a conversation with a chemist who retired recently from a big pharmaceutical company, I learned that science is on the brink of a new treatment that can link the chemotherapy to certain proteins, and thus will not have to be systemic (system-wide, including hair and nails and everything.) It is only a matter of time before this would be available.

I read about tests to intersperse chemotherapy and radiation treatments. My plan was now simply to use these treatments to buy time until something better was invented. Since I was having to cut out some one of the chemo threesome due to the allergic reaction I had a great plan to quit chemo for six weeks and get radiation. Then, I planned to come back and get chemo again, to finish up. I was so sure that Dr. Apple would love this plan that I didn't even prepare for a week of jello and applesauce. This was truly a hope beyond hope. It was a plan.

Dr. Apple's answer: "No, that would not be a full treatment. You need a full treatment."

I asked "Why?"

Dr. Apple answered, "A full treatment is the right course to follow."

I asked again, "But why is it better to do six chemo treatments all in a row, then radiation, than three chemo treatments and radiation then finish up the 'full treatment' of the chemo?"

Dr. Apple answered, "It is how we do it. Why do you keep asking?"

I explained to him, "It is probably the same course of treatment for the same disease, that left my cousin dead. Why don't we try something different?" I had said the word "dead." It hit the doctor like a blow from a fist. He clearly did not want to discuss "dead." He probably didn't want to talk about "passing on," or "entering the afterlife" or any other word for the big exit. I felt like I had used profanity in front of a child.

Dr. Apple argued, "You don't know anything about another person's case. Another person's case doesn't matter to you. What does matter is what we learn from thousands of cases."

I felt bogged down in stagnate reasoning. If we are not allowed to use one example, with a name and a face, why can we use a thousand examples we do not know? I tried a new direction. I explained, "Not only do I need to do better than my cousin, I also need to try something new to promise my daughter that she was born into a life better than mine. This was, after all, the breast that nurtured her through infancy and accompanied the lullabies and words of comfort I gave her. As she clung to this breast I told her, 'do not be afraid, life is good.'"

Dr. Apple answered, "Breast feeding has nothing to do with passing on breast cancer. It is genetic."

He was right, of course. But the point was, that it was the genetic nature that concerned me. I argued again, "I know it is genetic, and that is why, when my grandmother died, and my cousin died, and now I have it too, I want something better for my daughter. I don't want to do just what they did, I want to try something new." Opps, there was that "death" thing again. It just slipped out. But Dr. Apple was clearly distraught.

Dr. Apple assured me, "one in nine women gets breast cancer. So you have to expect family members to have it."

Now the mathematics were speaking on my behalf. "In my mother's family there were nine women. My grandmother, her three daughters, and her five granddaughters. That is nine women, and three have this aggressive form of cancer that kills people. Three in nine is more than statistics expect."

Dr. Apple concluded, "You have got to stop worrying about these things you know nothing about."

And so Dr. Apple left, and Laura came in, and proceeded with the fourth installment of this standard treatment. This time they tried leaving out the Cytoxen. And this time I was not allergic to the drugs.

Dr. Apple went out to the waiting room and took Tom aside (where I couldn't hear them conspiring.) He suggested to Tom I was "obsessed with death." So when Tom came in he asked if I wanted to see a counselor to help me through this crisis. It just happened that a cancer counselor was scheduled to come to the little monthly cancer seminars that the hospital offered, so I signed up to take part in the group discussion about "grief," the topic for the month.

I do care what Tom thinks of my mental state. I wanted to explain that I am not really obsessed with death. Actually I feel more obsessed with life, now that I have made this huge commitment to hold onto it. That does not mean I am afraid of "death." In fact, loving life, and fearing death are not opposites. You can love life, without being afraid of death at all. One actually enhances the other. Life is more beautiful when it is not totally centrifugally connected to the fear of losing it, and death is far less ferocious when life is good and complete.

CHAPTER 4

Another Bad Day

May, 1997

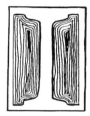 was barely on my feet again, less than a week from that fourth treatment, when my vague memories of the book of Job started reverberating through my life.

A sheriff's car idled in the driveway, and the officer at the door served me with a lawsuit. The papers were a meshwork of legal jargon, and the butterfly netted in that meshwork was my own self image as a "good person." I am always the "good guy" in the stories I know about myself. How could anyone want to sue me?

A year before, as I was driving to work one beautiful spring day, my old grey diesel car was just sauntering along at 30 miles per hour in a 40 m.p.h. zone. No one was around to hurry me, or to honk because I was slowing traffic, so I slowed to that comfortable speed. When I came to the entrance where I was to turn, there still were no cars behind me, so I stopped before turning left. I was in no hurry, since I was twenty minutes early for work. I always allow time for more traffic. Suddenly, out of nowhere a car appeared square in front of me. I guess we were both startled to see each other. She reacted by slamming on her brakes. Her brakes locked up and her car skidded and out of control, off the road, barely missing a telephone pole and a tree. Then it hurdled into the parked cars at the far end of the parking lot into which I had been turning.

I drove into the lot, in slow motion, still dazed by the incident I had just witnessed. Before I could even pull into a space the driver of that now wrecked car was running toward me, yelling obscenities, telling me I had caused the accident. She called the police on her cell phone.

I asked her if she was alright. And I was relieved to see she was not hurt. Her car, and the car she hit were badly damaged.

The police officer came and took all the information. Even though I was not charged, I kept reviewing the mishap in my mind. I could think of nothing I could have done to prevent it. Yet for weeks afterward I lay awake nights recalling that car, hurdling out of nowhere, and the woman shouting accusations at me, and me not even having a dent to make me "pay for it." It was definitely a justice thing.

As I drove over that road again, and thought through the chain of events, it was apparent what had happened. I was unfamiliar with the road. I had never driven further than the driveway to the parking lot where I turned left. I was unaware of a dip in the road, just beyond the driveway which created a blind spot. The road was perfectly straight, and the dip was deep enough to hide a car, so the center line appeared to be continuous making the dip even more invisible. Hence I think we were taken by surprise. I was stopped because there was no traffic, and I could afford to stop. I felt she may have been driving a little faster because there was no traffic. I replayed that over and over again at the time. Now, with this lawsuit in hand, I started replaying it again and again this year.

My insurance company was sending a lawyer to talk with me on May 14.

On the night of May 13, the night before I talked with the lawyer, I had a dream that I saw that accident again. But this time the car was different. It was a blue car, not a gold car. And in this dream it missed the telephone pole, but it hit the tree. In this dream, the woman didn't jump out of the car yelling at me. I opened the door of the car, and two people were in the car, pale-white and lifeless. There was such an eerie stillness it woke me.

The next morning I told the lawyer I was still having nightmares. I wanted this thing resolved as quickly as possible. He assured me that I really wanted it to take years. Things were just going badly all around, and I wanted to be done with problems.

A few days before, on May 9, the same morning that I had been served with the lawsuit, my father had called, and his voice sounded strangely flat. Dad was the person for whom the term "eternal optimist" was invented. He always had an incessantly cheerful sound to his "hello" regardless of any circumstances good or bad. Yet on this day he sounded like an old man.

He told me he needed radiation for a recurrence of prostate cancer. Surgery was his cancer cure, and I knew radiation frightened him.

When I asked questions like, how was it diagnosed? He wasn't sure, but thought it must have been a blood test because that was the only test he had been given. I asked him what kind of radiation. He didn't know anything at all about it. I asked him how long would the treatments go on. He said "five weeks starting today."

Today? That means there was no time to find these answers and put his mind at ease over all this. "Why today?" I asked. He said "That's when they could start."

I had been reading up on radiation, since it was part of my plan to survive, so I suggested, "Find out if it is cobalt or linear accelerator, and if they don't have the up-to-date equipment then think about coming here for it." We have a guest room. We could do that easily. He said he would check on it. I sent him my little booklet on radiation therapy from the National Cancer Institute.

I called him back after he had a chance to talk with his doctor some more. That was Tuesday, May 13. He sounded much more upbeat. I had a long phone visit with both Mom and Dad which left me feeling very happy and peaceful although not much news passed between us. I think we had said everything there was to say.

The next evening, May 14, I went to the "grief" seminar for cancer patients or, as we were euphemistically titled, "Cancer Survivors."

Personally I would prefer to be called "Cancer Livers," since survival seems a lot less qualitative than living, and cancer has that characteristic of underscoring the qualitative aspects of life, rather than the quantitative. But I imagine titling people with a disease is the task of the medical community, and for them, "Cancer Liver" is a biological thing, and "Surviving" is a worthy ultimate goal.

The gathering of women included several familiar faces, people I had seen at other cancer survivor events. We were all round faced white women with unusual hair.

A tall, kind, and hairless woman brought a lot of cancer books, all much newer than those in our local library. She opened the seminar by asking us to list what we had lost due to cancer. That was an easy assignment for me. I had thought a lot about that. I had lost my fear of cancer. I had lost my fear of doctors, and medicine, and stainless steel. I had lost my secret fear of losing people I loved, because cancer gave me an opportunity to talk with those I love in ultimate, significant terms. I had lost the sense of eternity in the words "till death due us part." And so my marriage was more focused. We had lost money. I had lost hair, and beauty. I had traded the word "hope" for "plan" in my conversation, so one might say, I had lost "hope."

I couldn't help but think of my gains as well. I had gained lots of time. Time that was always wasted plotting the mundane now became precious time. I had lots and lots of life time to put things in perspective, and appreciate friends and family as I never had before. After all, the other side of a slow death is a long life. The "C" word, as it is known in circles of denial, is an "EXCUSED"stamp across all that is unimportant. It offers a chance to re-prioritize things, and realize that earning $7.25 an hour is not as important as having lunch with a friend.

I finished my list, and looked up to see Tom and Mariah standing in the doorway of this meeting room. They both had tears streaming down their faces. My only thought was how thankful I was to see both of them alive and well amid this obvious tragic moment. I excused myself from the "grief" meeting to begin the journey into actual grief.

Tom said, "There has been an accident." My mind flashed back to the traffic accident nightmare I had the night before. I saw the car was a familiar blue Saturn, and I saw the two people in the car. Tom went on to put words to the picture. "Your mom was driving. They went off the road, and into a tree. They were both killed." The dream that had left me with the awful empty feeling escorted my visual senses right through the denial stage of grief. I knew I would not awaken from this. I was already awake. The message was "Call Jack."

I looked at Mariah. This beautiful young woman offering me comfort would never know the comfort of having a sibling at a time like this. I thought of Jack, my brother, who, even though we are years and miles from one another, exactly shares my feelings at this moment.

In the hours between the phone conversation with him and his actual arrival at our house we connected every thread of our familial ties. We called all of Mom's and Dad's brothers and sisters. We repeated the tragic words again and again, as a mantra setting us on a new course of grief.

An hour before Jack's expected arrival at our house an administrator of Mariah's school called. She sounded distressed, and said she had to talk to me right away. I told her I was just preparing to leave for New York. She said it was imperative that we talk right now. Could I come to her office? I really wanted to hear whatever it was from Mariah first before I went into a situation where I might have to defend her. I made arrangements to go to the school and meet Mariah, then together we would see this administrator.

When I met Mariah at the door of the school she explained that she had loaned her assignment book to a friend, to give her that day's assignment. But the friend looked through the book, and found Mariah's page of resolutions she had made the first day of school that year. It included the goal, "to not commit suicide." So that is what we were going to talk about.

Mariah tried to explain to the school official that she had written down this goal because she meant what it said. And that was all.

"But why would a high school junior, at the top of her class, with everything going for her, even think of such a thing?" The high school administrator knew that the statistics for teen suicides were very high among these bright and talented young people, as well as I did.

Some parents and children share their secrets, secretly. The child hides the diary, and the parent sneaks in and reads it. But in our family, we don't practice this kind of obligatory spying. With our particular personalities choosing times for personal privacy and times for personal openness leaves a wider doorway to conversation. So I had not read Mariah's personal journals, and I did not know if she had a large collection of suicide notes tucked under her mattress. I also had not read this assignment book that the school administrator had found. But when I heard it, I took it as a positive note that she would not commit suicide.

Even though I do not read her journals, we do spend many hours of conversation together and I was aware that she had considered suicide as an option. When she was only about nine or ten years old, I knew that she felt weighed down with heavy issues. We often had long in-depth conversations while on walks. She talked about people killing themselves. I knew she was looking for options. I also knew that these concerns were not unusual for gifted children. It was hard to think of what to say. The options that crossed my mind were: "Never talk about that again." "We love you, so you are required to survive for us." "Yes, I have heard of that, what have you heard?" (I think the third choice is the right one, however, I probably laid option number two on her, either spoken or unspoken, I don't remember.)

Tom and I took it as a serious concern and a significant issue. We started the search for a counselor. That project was complicated by the fact that Tom was a pastor, and the circle of people with whom we could share this concern was very small. We sat in several waiting rooms and several offices before we found someone who was not scarier than her problem. Finding the right person to talk to is a very personal decision, and a lot harder than picking out a new car or a new hair style. I imagine most people have to try several, but it is well worth the trouble.

During this time I also talked with her gifted teacher, and the teacher recommended some books to her. Mariah found *The Gifted Kids Survival Guide,*[11] by Judy Galbraith, helpful because it dealt with several things that were pressuring her and offered positive tools for problem solving. And finally we did find a counselor who talked with Mariah. As the elements of wisdom and understanding filled in some voids, Mariah explained to me that suicide was an option in problem solving. But it is not a very useful option because it closes out all the other options.

Now, here we were, again, facing the "S" word. I explained to the school administrator that in our household we talk openly about such things because we can't make them not

---

[11]This is actually two books, *The Gifted Kids Survival Guide for Ages 10 & Under,*(Copyright© 1984) and *The Gifted Kids Survival Guide (For Ages 11-18)* (Copyright© 1983) both by Judy Galbraith, Free Spirit Publishing Company, Minneapolis, MN.

exist by pretending no one thinks of them. So when Mariah came here as a sophomore and found that entering a new school in a whole new cultural setting was difficult, she applied her problem solving skills. She examined all the alternatives. After thinking about suicide she chose life. As she began her junior year, Mariah feared her rigorous academic program, and she was still dealing with the social adjustment, so she set down some guidelines for her own problem solving. And that was what was written in this book.

The woman returned the book to Mariah. And we were excused to go back to the reality of death. I felt grateful the school was sensitive to this issue, but the timing left much to be desired.

Inheritance

Mom and Dad were always so proud of Jack, and because they kept me tuned into Jack's every deed and accomplishment, he and I had a remote control type of relationship over the years. Now I was feeling we had sort of lost sight of each other. I knew Jack was a single "self-made" kind of guy. He was half owner of a business that published an advertising paper. He had a pilot's license, (but did not own a plane). He did own several large boats though, since one of his side-lines included restoring wooden sailboats and speedboats.

One of his boats once won a "best in show" at a boat show sponsored by the Yacht Club in Orient, New York, where my parents had many friends. That was certainly one of our dad's proudest moments.

Jack lived near Detroit on Lake St. Clair, and he was engaged to his girlfriend of several years. They planned to be married in September, so even though I have always pictured him as kind of a loner, I knew he was not completely alone. I wondered what he would be like as executor of Mom and Dad's estate. Would he remember the art, and poetry, and the spiritual grace that surrounded our parent's lives? Or would he focus on their inability to make sensible business deals?

A generation ago we watched this issue of inheritance being played out in my mother's family. My mother's father, Harry C. Munro was a very brilliant college professor -- teacher of theology, and Christian education. He was a "flower child" before flower children were invented in the 60's, and long before they became so worldly as to take drugs. He was an idealist through and through. He wore home-made clothes because in the 40's men's shirts did not come from the store in stained glass window patterns. He whistled union rally songs, because in the 50's the musical rallying cries for civil rights hadn't yet been strummed. He credited God with touching everything with grace. And he spent his life proving God's goodness on earth.

Grandpa Munro chose a piece of the Michigan sand dunes, on the shore of the lake, to call our family home. Our family was mostly pastors and other wanderers who were spread across this continent, so it was fitting that our family land should be a summer gathering place.

Before his death Grandpa Munro divided the land into parcels and assumed his children and grandchildren would share with one another, and would always provide a place for his new wife whom we called Aunt Dot. Grandpa, being a full fledged idealist, seemed totally oblivious to normal human behavior. I am sure he assumed the selfish side of human nature did not apply to his family since we all were, in his eyes, destined for sainthood. But in real life a designated place for Aunt Dot was not written down in legal words. What may have seemed to Grandpa a guarantee of her inclusion in the life of the family, in reality became a closed door leaving her out of the family property altogether.

Mom felt that Aunt Dot needed a place at Duneswood, so she "gave" her our cottage, which was sort of stacked on the side of a sand dune under the cottage built by Mom's sister, Ginnie. Since Aunt Ginnie and Aunt Dot lived near each other in winter months, and traveled north together from Texas, that seemed a good arrangement. With that agreement, I am sure, there was a financial reconciliation as well since my parents were always in dire financial need.

But when Mom and Dad saw how ownership of property by "birthright" tore families asunder they promised us, "you will never have any inheritance but your love for one another. Don't let money separate you from your inheritance." I know parents always think that is understood, but Mom and Dad actually did say it with words. And they carried it out by actually having nothing for us to quibble about.

As the years passed the ownership tensions over Duneswood continued. So too did the natural movement of the earth. Sand dunes are like a giant conveyor belt moving ever so slowly toward the sea. The one hundred year old pine Mom focused on to prove our house and plot would not be washed away in one hundred years was actually moving, roots and all, closer and closer to the lake. So building our cottage next to the old tree may have seemed like a good plan. But the house, being heavier than the pine tree, and much less flexible, fell faster. I think it crashed into the lake around the time that Aunt Dot remarried and chose not to go there anymore.

Going back after many years, looking down the bank at the rubble, the ruins of the cottage that my parents, and my brother and I built, I am reminded of the lesson in this symbol: The only inheritance one can really claim is spiritual. For that, I am grateful.

You don't really have to be a mystic to realize that money is actually the most imaginary tangible thing around. It only has value if people believe in it. And yet a person who bases goals on obtaining money is considered a realist. A person who chooses a life based on spiritual treasures is thought to be an idealist. Odd isn't it? In truth the physical world is a mere symbol of the spiritual reality. Perhaps I would not think this way if I had money. I don't know. It's not likely I'll put myself in a position to find out. I really wondered, though, where Jack's beliefs lay, now that he was a business entrepreneur.

Jack flew to our house in a borrowed plane. It came with a pilot for the return trip. Then Jack and I drove on to Greenport, Long Island. The four and half hour car trip was a reacquainting time.

Jack had grown gray and wise. He was living in a complicated, competitive world filled with credit cards and the most up-to-date technology. When I last knew him as a person, (a quarter of a century ago) he was a smart little kid with Buddy Holly glasses who liked to tinker with cars and boats. I asked him if he was still a "fix-it" guy.

He assured me he was. Now, however, he fixes anything that goes wrong, be it computers, delivery trucks, or disputes between employers or even competitors. When he brought up the subject of people getting along with people we headed straight into what concerned both of us most. Did we each remember what our inheritance was supposed to be? Jack picked it up. "Mom and Dad promised to leave us nothing material. Our only inheritance was our ability to be a family together through grief." I didn't have to say it for it to be spoken.

It was no surprise to find that their house was just newly second mortgaged, and there was no sign of life insurance anywhere. The money Mom and Dad had just borrowed last month was nearly gone. Everything tangible was in the form of art, and poetry. Even the furniture in their little home-made house qualified as art. The files were very clear and easy to find— color coded: red for banking and finances; black for death, complete with a pre-written memorial service. Dad's encounters with cancer over the years had brought them openly to this precipice between life and death many times. They acknowledged death as a possibility, but they always chose life.

On the table in their studio was a letter they had copied hundreds of times until the toner ran out on the copier. And on their computer was a mailing list of 400 friends who should receive this letter. They sent these tomes out to all their friends and family several times a year. Keeping in touch with people was their life. I know they had agonized over limiting the list to just 400. Since that was the number determined by the price of stamps and their tight budget.

Jack read the letter, then he gave it to me. I read it, then I read it aloud. Half laughing and half crying we passed the letter back and forth reading one paragraph again and again.

"I think I haven't written to anyone since Valentine's Day. Time flies, so I will give you a rundown on what has been happening. As most of you know, after Milt wrecked the car some time at the end of last year, I decided we'd go everywhere together with me doing most of the driving. He is a much better driver, of course, but he gets to thinking about other things. We have found that we both sort of need each other."

Each time we read over the concluding paragraph we could hear Mom cheerfully finalizing a letter wrought with fears and frustrations— Dad's cancer, my cancer, the city ordinance requiring they fence their yard due to their garden fish pond, etc.

"Actually, I know this letter sounds down but we are in very good spirits, and so thankful for the prayers and love of so many wonderful people. It is so beautiful here now with the water so blue, and all the flowering trees in bloom. Life seems basically wonderful and beautiful and we all feel very 'up'. So keep us in your prayers, but do not feel sorry for us, for we are going through experiences which are most precious and enriching."

In the weeks to come, I took the mailing list and edited the letter into one that would inform their friends, and sent it out. Hundreds of letters came from all over the country to Jack and me, each sharing personal experiences that they had with Mom and Dad. It was tremendously helpful.

Jack and I spent the week between lawyer visits, memorial events, teas, dinners, etc. pouring over their files of poems, prayers, stories, artwork, and just standing in awe of their rich, spiritual lives.

The first few days we made numerous telephone calls to Aunt Ginnie in Texas, because she knew things that we never knew we would need to know, and because her voice offered us a familiar sense of peace and well-being.

She knew all the things about where to begin when death leaves you alone on life's shore. She had been twice a widow. She was also the strong presence when Grandpa died, and then when Aunt Dot's second husband passed away, and then, when Aunt Dot died. She knew to clean out the refrigerator first, and then to find the right lawyer. She walked us through all those things that must have been published somewhere in a "how to" book, but because death is the topic it would never have been read.

Perhaps, in the calm of her voice that we found a comfort, was hidden the pain and stress of her own loss of her sister. Aunt Ginnie did not answer her telephone. We tried calling at different times of the day. Finally, I heard from my cousin that she had stroke, and was hospitalized.

My mom had always felt especially close to Ginnie. Mom's answer to my childhood fears was to tell a family story about her own overcoming of fear. Mom told me she had always been afraid of the water. Learning to swim for her, was out of the question. As a child hearing that story I found it confusing because my mom was an excellent swimmer. She loved to swim. She had a lifeguard badge and pictures of herself as a lifeguard at a camp. I could not really accept that she had ever even known fear at all, if she was calling herself afraid of water.

Mom told me about how Ginnie, as a teenager, was in a terrible car accident. When she went to see her in the hospital she was frightened and shocked by the terrible devastation to this beautiful young girl. She begged her sister to get through this, and promised to give her "anything in the world" to show how much she cared for her. Well, Ginnie did ask her little sister for something. But it was not a material thing, as Mom was prepared to give. Ginnie asked Mom to learn to swim. And so she did. That was the end of fear. Never having seen my mother's fear, or having seen Aunt Ginnie with a less than perfect appearance I simply set this story aside. It stayed in the archives of my mind, until this day, when Mom's courage, and Aunt Ginnie's amazing ability to deal with rough times was something I needed to review.

Angels

Mom and Dad gave out extra keys to their house quite freely. But that didn't matter, since they rarely locked the doors. Dad always said, "you just don't know what people are going to bring in." And he was usually right about that. People were always bringing them things, like fresh fish, or garden produce, seedlings for their garden, or materials for projects for Mom's artistry.

We joked about the fact that the only time they were robbed was when Dad went sailing and left his wallet with money and credit cards on the dashboard of his car which was parked in the lot of the public marina. He did remember to lock the car. But he forgot to put the top up on the convertible. That happened many years ago when he could risk forgetfulness, without being accused of aging.

When Mom and Dad's fatal accident became public knowledge, and before we arrived in New York, Colin decided to secure the house. Colin was a neighbor whom Mom and Dad considered as a son even though he was much younger than Jack and I. He and his wife spent much time and shared many tears with us also.

While he was at their house he decided to mow their lawn. Jack and I arrived and found the lawn freshly mowed. Colin neatly avoided each of Dad's new little seedling trees which, in fifty years will make the yard a virtual forest. Through the tears and hugs Colin said, "What is a 79 year old man doing planting all those little tiny trees? Did they expect to grow old in the shade?"

Jack and I answered in near unison. We said they planted them for the children, of course, for the generations to come. We had heard Dad's "pioneer sermon" many times. For Mom and Dad mortality was another door to be left unlocked. They did not need to restrict life to their mortal lifetime. They were part of a whole on-going creation of human beings.

Jack and Colin went to the police station for the police report, and to photograph the wreck. The items that Jack and Colin retrieved from the wrecked car were: Mom's purse containing $9.00 and sewing kit, Dad's wallet with credit cards, (lots and lots of those) and from the backseat, the research for the artwork Mom was working on at the time. It was a large book of angels. Her artwork was shattered. Throughout the car, laid many of her little angel paintings.

I first met the angels when my grandmother died, when I was a small child. Grandpa Munro went to Duneswood, and each day for two months he poured a concrete step in a stairway going from the beach to the top of the dune where he and Grandma had a favorite spot for viewing the sunsets. He posted a sign, "The Bright Angel Trail, for Angel's only." As I flipped through the book of angels I thought of that stairway to heaven when each step was thigh high on me and I jumped from one to the next imagining Grandma as an angel, while Grandpa whistled, "Does the Moon Shine Tonight on Pretty Redwing."

I do not have to watch this kind of separation of my parents. That seems right in a way. They were always together. That was their life. That was their death. The backseat was full of angels. That was their life. That was their death.

I always thought that grief was a construct of sorrow. But now that I am here, I find that it is the happy moments that leave me feeling alone. Mom and Dad were the people we called when we needed to share our joys: Mariah's acceptance to Governors's school — Tom's brilliant sermons ideas — this beautiful season of springtime — a new recipe — all these wonderful people that surround us — little successes and achievements — happy moments are what feel most hollow in a time of loss.

Jack and I called and wrote to everyone for whom Mom and Dad had an address or telephone number. Finally their phone stopped ringing with friends, and only the telemarketers were left ringing the house. I started getting a little more blunt when I answered. Jack overheard me on the phone with the chimney sweep (they didn't have a fireplace.) I was saying, "Don't call back because they are dead." He encouraged me to be more tactful.

We recalled the old joke Dad often repeated about the traveler who called his family and asked his brother, "How's my cat?" The stay at home brother answered, "The cat is dead." The traveling sibling said "Oh no! Couldn't you have been more sensitive? I mean couldn't you help me through it little by little, like saying the cat is on the roof. Then the next time I call say "The cat fell off the roof and got hurt." Then you can say, "Gee, we tried to save her, but she died." The stay at home brother understood. He promised to keep that in mind. Then the long traveling brother asked, "How's Mom?" The brother answered, "She's on the roof."

The next time the phone rang, Jack answered. I reminded him, "Now say 'she is on the roof.'" But this time he was blunt. "Well, Mom is dead, and so is Dad." I said, "How can you be so insensitive? You just told me to be more tactful, even to the chimney sweep telemarketer." He said, "well, that was Mom's psychic. She said she was worried about Mom. What's she doing using the telephone? What kind of psychic is that?"

The Memorial Service was at Orient. That was where Mom and Dad had wanted us to have it. Dad, in addition to his newspaper column and radio show, also worked as an interim pastor. He filled in at churches that were in search of a new pastor. As a result he had recently pastored several churches within the fifty mile radius of their home. Each of the churches assumed he was their own pastor. Orient, the smallest of the churches, was different. Dad had served at the Orient church as their regular full time pastor for about eight years after his official retirement from the business of producing religious and educational media materials. Mom and Dad then moved to Ohio to be near us during Mariah's childhood years. As we talked of moving, they took the opportunity to have this house built on a lot in Greenport, near Orient, which they considered their beloved home. So we were sure that Orient was the right place for a service.

Tom and Mariah came out to Greenport. The problem was, our extended families were mostly located in Illinois, Texas, Michigan and Minnesota. None of their brothers or sisters or nieces and nephews, no relatives, except us, were able to make a speedy trip through New York City, to the most remote point on Long Island. The lodgings for visitors are expensive beach fronts that require much advance planning to even consider.

So we found ourselves in a very strange situation. Several churches and communities were grieving for our parents. But we, the family, barely knew anyone. The surroundings were very beautiful, but strange to us. Hundreds of people came to the various events, but all they knew of Mom and Dad they had learned in the very recent years. It was like our parents began their lives when most people are shutting down and moving to Florida.

We decided to accumulate missing pieces from the local services and put into a mid-western memorial service to be held at a time more convenient to the extended family who could not come to New York. Having that to look forward to was very helpful to me, and I think to our family.

The Boat They Called "Mariah"

One evening while we were having dinner, Mariah just blurted out, "I want the boat." Mom and Dad had a wooden dinghy with a sail. Dad used it as his token boat so he could belong to the Yacht Club where people got together, which was what he really liked to do most. Jack, who restores wooden boats, had always taken care of that dinghy. He was really the only one who had ever taken it out on the water.

When we went to the house it was not there. Jack searched for it and found it up on sawhorses behind the garage of a friend who had helped Mom and Dad move. It probably never actually got moved into their new home. We could see that claiming it was going to a bit sticky. I could see Jack really wanted it. I explained to Mariah that Jack would have to have the dinghy. She insisted it was hers. Her name was on it. True, Mom and Dad had named it "Mariah." Most sailboats named "Mariah" are named after the wind. But this "Mariah" was definitely named for her. I tried to explain she already had stuff with her name on it. And what would she ever do with a boat? I tried to reason that Jack has boat trailers and a boat house and waterfront property. He knows how to sail boats. We don't even rent row-boats at the reservoir. We could, but we don't.

She insisted it was hers. I've never heard her sound so greedy before. When she was twelve years old Mariah wanted only money for Christmas. Then she sent all she received to a project in the Third World to help families receive livestock and education on caring for the animals. She babysat as a young teen. And every penny she earned she sent off to help someone else. She wrote stories and editorials to make people aware of other's needs. It never crossed my mind that she had her eye on Mom and Dad's material wealth, such as it was. She doesn't ask for clothes or C-D's, or any of the usual "kid things." But here she wants this big, useless (to her) thing that is going to be a big problem to get. I was very annoyed with her attitude, and I told her that. Tom just calmly let it go by. When we reached the shouting stage Tom called me aside and said "Can't you see this is part of grief. She is not really being selfish and unreasonable. She wants her grandparents to call her by name."

Guided by Tom's gentle wisdom I went back to the discussion. It was not about a boat. It was about her grandparents. Then Mariah said what we were all feeling. "So many friends claimed them as though they were family. We were just sort of 'in the way' at the Memorial Service." It was for friends, not family. She felt like no one cared that she was important to them. The boat was a symbol to her, that they cared about her. After we talked about this we decided a fair exchange to owning a boat was for her to know that she would be included in the memorial service we were planning for family.

I wonder how many people have asked for sail boats when what they really needed was a chance to write a eulogy? Mariah has a gift for putting words to feelings. Yet, I think of all the times I have thought I longed for sailboats and seacoasts with visible horizon, when what I have really wanted was a blank page, a pen and a thought.

As it turned at the Memorial Service held the next year Mariah read the benediction which was her grandfather's prayer written for the Orient Yacht club "The Blessing of the Fleet." She went with Jack to Michigan for a sailing lesson and a visit with the boat named Mariah, that he is keeping for her.

Getting Done with Chemo

Each treatment normally includes the CA27-29 blood test before I get the chemo drugs. Being an interested participant in this whole thing, I usually don't wait for Dr. Apple to come in and tell me the results of the test. As soon as I am able to make phone calls after each treatment I call up his office, and ask for the test results. I have found that if the results are good, (like they were after my 3rd treatment, tested at the time of the 4th treatment,) they tell me right away. But the information is not a readily forth-coming if it is negative. The test at the 5th treatment would tell if my good feelings lately were a true indicator of winning the cancer battle, or if I was just feeling the effects of no allergic reaction to the drugs.

Having so many other things going on in May I had little time to prepare myself for this treatment. So at the last minute before treatment began, I panicked and threw up while Laura was just getting ready to insert the needle. Later, when I called in and asked for CA27-29 test results and Dr. Apple's nurse said I was not tested this time, I was not surprised.

June, 1997

When I signed in at the M.O.U. in June for treatment number six, my last, I promised Laura I was better prepared. She would be able to take the blood for the CA27-29 this time without me throwing up in her face. Laura said, "What do you mean? We did the CA27-29 test last time." I said, "I called for the results, and the nurse said it was not done." Laura said, "of course it was done. It was 40." What had been 32 after the first treatment, 30 after the second, and 25 after the third, was now 40. (37 is the high end of normal.) Even though the treatments were much easier without the allergic reaction it obviously wasn't working. Or perhaps all the stress with my parent's death was to blame. My plan for winning the cancer battle seemed futile. All this time and money and trouble and my cancer is only slightly less obvious than it was when it was a full sized tumor popping out of my breast. I know these little discouragements are the name of the game when it comes to cancer, but I really wasn't prepared for it. The last treatment is supposed to be a time of celebration, and completion. I only felt disappointment.

Having cancer is like being chased by a bear. You can make lots of choices along the way. You can choose to be eaten or to run. Of course the bear can run faster. So if you choose to run you can choose to keep running and eventually get eaten. Or, you can try something spectacular like climbing a tree. From the safe spot in the tree you can get a perspective on the situation. You see that the bear is at the bottom of the tree trunk. That is the only trunk this tree has. That is the trunk you had planned to climb down, when you thought of a plan. Then you remember a science special on bears on P.B.S. A cheerful guy in a safari jacket says, "Despite their large size, bears are excellent climbers."

Well, there is always the chance that the bear may get bored and wander away, or it may go to sleep at the bottom of the tree. That would be safe enough. But, with a sleeping bear at the base of the tree, coming down would be no easier. If the bear climbs up you could climb higher. Or you could jump out of the tree, to be chased on the ground again, assuming you hadn't broken any bones in the jump that would preclude running. So you climb higher. The jump option becomes more dangerous. The branches are thinning, barely supporting you. You still have choices. You can jump from the top of the tree and break your neck. Or you can get eaten by the bear. There are always choices.

I glanced over the pages of this journal as I waited for Dr. Apple to come and tell me the official medical version of the bad news. I was reminded by the journal that when I went into this I was really only buying time. I was simply climbing the tree. I got time. Here, sixth months later I am no worse than when I started. Without the treatment I would certainly be worse. I was concerned I might be allergic to the drugs, and the stem cell therapy would be more destructive than I was prepared for. And sure enough, when and if I do need stem cell therapy I will know to tell them to avoid cytoxen. So, I have gained something in the way of knowledge about myself. Maybe I have gained enough time that stem cell therapy would be covered by my insurance. Maybe, despite the bad news, maybe I can deal with this.

My dialogue with Dr. Apple confirmed these choices. If more tests showed more cancer I could have more chemo — like I had, or I could try something new, like stem cell therapy and the same chemo. Or, I could just be eaten by the bear. Since radiation treatment was next on my dance card, and this was Dr. Tallhouse's domain, and Dr. Tallhouse provides so much clarity, I decided I would just keep right on clinging to this branch and singing all the bear lullabies that came to mind.

CHAPTER 5

A Thread of Truth

ilt and Rosie met at church camp. Rosie spent her college summers working on the camp staff, while Milt, as a young seminary student was a group leader. Rosie tells of sitting in on a discussion he was leading. As he took the group deeper and deeper into his intellectual encounters with theology and philosophy, Milt was only slightly distracted by a small thread hanging down from his hat. Being a first year seminary student (whose hormones were probably exuding theological platitudes in place of phonemes) a misplaced hat thread posed a threat to his dignity. It demanded subtle, but immediate attention. As he talked, he tugged at the thread. The thread did not break. It only became longer until it could wrap around his hand several times. He continued to talk while pie shaped pieces of fabric began dropping off his head in all directions as his hat disintegrated. Rosie loved repeating that story. Now here I am, tampering with my father's dignity also, telling that story just to make an analogy.

As Jack and I began unraveling the details about the car crash the thread of truth came loose from a collection of wedge shaped pieces of understanding I used to wear like a hat. The hat pieces had names like "blame," "retaliation," and "justice." As we pulled the lose thread all of these protective wedges fell randomly around us at our feet in a chaotic pattern of right and wrong. They were seemingly determined by nothing but gravity.

We took hold of the thread that led us through the sequence of events at the time when we first heard of the car crash. Actually, Jack had a picture of the whole story on the day of the accident. It began when he saw the officer standing at the door of his house as he returned from work on that particular Wednesday. He, like me in my dream, had a premonition of the accident. In his premonition Mom and Dad were driving along when something went wrong, and Dad reached for the steering wheel. He was looking out the passenger side of the windshield as they came upon a telephone pole. He missed the telephone pole, but did not see the tree they hit a few feet beyond the pole. He was not protected by his seatbelt because he was reaching for the steering wheel while sitting oddly in his seat.

The officer said to Jack, "Your parents were killed when their car veered off the road and into a tree." Jack asked right then, what it would take to have an autopsy done and impound the car. He learned that the car was already impounded on the police lot in Riverhead. He wanted my agreement to have an autopsy done. I agreed to the autopsy because he seemed unsettled about the cause. I thought it would help put the issue to rest. I was sure they would find that Mom had a heart attack or something. I felt the cause of the accident had to lie in the fact that something was suddenly wrong with Mom. I reasoned that their wish to donate their organs could not be honored due to Mom's probable heart attack and Dad's recurrence of cancer. I thought, therefore, an autopsy would be a good idea.

As we got together, we talked about the dreams and premonitions we had each had. Even before we heard any factual information our pictures seemed eerily the same. The air bag was unfurled in Mom's lap. Dad was reaching over with his right hand to take the steering wheel. In my dream they were frozen in time in this position. In Jack's picture it was an animated sequence of events. In his picture he included every little mechanical detail, right down to the deployment of the air bag. The similarities of our perception amazed us in such a way that we felt it was imperative to do something. What to do was not at all clear. We started pulling the string unraveling whatever facts we could.

Believe It Or Not

These things, I think, seem to elicit that atonal whistled background music that accompanies science fiction. My various, recent brushes with actual science have done nothing to curb these ways of perceiving. I still believe that God not only exists, but is a conspicuous and active part of all of our daily lives. We have to go to great imaginary lengths to close God out. Separation from God is a skill that takes practice. It is not something with which we are born. That is why children are capable of deep prayers and spiritual understanding and adults have trouble finding God, even when they need God.

"Miracles," "mystical occurrences" and "the metaphysical" are some of the tabloid adjectives used in our culture to talk about spiritual encounters. These are great words. They say what they mean. But in our culture they imply an oddity about spiritual encounters that says the human race is separated into groups that apply these special words to their lives and people who do not. Really all people, I think, are constantly exposed to a very "in your face" God who loves us. Encounters with God are natural, not supernatural. They are normal, not paranormal.

I believe that God spoke to me in a dream, and to Jack in a premonition. I believe God probably spoke to Mom and

Dad too. God meant to tell us that this car crash was a physical (scientific) inevitability. Mom and Dad made phone calls to loved ones and completed their conversations on earth. Jack and I saw the details of this accident. For some reason, known only to God, I suppose, we were called to use this knowledge. But we know that no actual, sensible adult human being is going to listen to a dream and a premonition. So it was imperative that we get the best scientific take on it that we could.

Jack and Colin went to the scene of the crash and to the police impound lot while I worked on funeral arrangements. Jack publishes an automotive advertising newspaper. He has lots of experience taking explicit photos of cars. He took lots of pictures of every conceivable aspect of the wrecked car. He took photos of the tree and the road. He included photos of how the road looked to Mom and Dad in their last moments of life. They took the film to a one hour processing place. That evening he entered his notes on his laptop. He reported that the windshield of the car was broken in such a way that confirmed our picture of Dad reaching across to take the steering wheel.

We created a list of all the possible things that could have happened. Rosie could have fallen asleep or had a heart attack. I thought she probably had a heart attack, since, had she fallen asleep Milt would not have leaned forward and reached for the steering wheel, but would have awakened her. Also the car driving behind them was not alerted to any sleepy, or out of control driving patterns. We considered the possibility that something was in the road or another car caused them to maneuver out of the way. But the police report included a statement from a witness who put those possibilities aside. One by one each possible scenario was discounted. It seemed that only something wrong with the driver or the car would explain why the car just drove off the road into a tree. It was not even a special, unique or isolated tree. It was just a gnarly old sycamore in a row of several on the edge of a field of grass in the vineyard area of Long Island. Had she planned it, Mom certainly would have chosen a special tree, one that was an easy target. This one was obscured by a telephone pole. Early afternoon on a bright sunny, spring day what else could go so wrong? Had she planned it, she would not have used a car with a driver's side air bag, and she probably would have driven faster than thirty-five or forty miles per hour. She probably would not have chosen to cross the road into another lane of traffic. We were certain that their "love of life" attitude prevailed to their last breaths.

A day or two later Jack and Colin and I stopped at the Riverhead Hospital where Mom and Dad had been taken and where they both died. We went to pick up some of the personal things that they had with them, that were not left in the car.

I was expecting to get Mom's diamond ring and her wedding band. I had never seen her without these rings. I really wanted to have them even though they were of very little value. Mom's diamond was very small and, she was quick to point out, it was flawed. Their engagement, like their marriage, was frugal. But when the hospital personnel handed us their things the rings were missing. It seemed odd to think they would have been stolen, since all their other valuables were readily accounted for. Mom's purse, and Dad's wallet were with the car until Jack and Colin retrieved them. The personal items we received at the hospital included Dad's watch which actually was more valuable than Mom's rings. Where were Mom's rings?

The doctor who had been on duty in the emergency room when they were brought in came out to talk with us. She was very candid. We really appreciated that. I thought surely we could confirm that Mom had a heart attack or stroke. But she said Rosie did not show signs of a stroke or heart attack. They were both alive and their vital signs were encouraging enough that they sent for a helicopter to take them on to a bigger hospital. But there was nothing they could do. Rosie's's injuries were typical of severe blunt force trauma. Milton died first, and five minutes later, Rosie died. The doctor added, "Obviously she wasn't wearing a seat belt...."

I was astounded! Mom, not wearing a seatbelt? That is impossible! Suddenly I could feel my temper flaring because something was wrong with the truth here. Mom chose this car because she was a seatbelt fanatic. We had seatbelts installed in cars when they were just an airplane thing.

One time, probably the only time, in her adult life she did not wear a seatbelt was before cars had belts in the backseats. She was relegated to the back seat because they were driving an older woman who could not climb in and out as easily. When Mom realized she would have no seatbelt in the back she offered to wait until Dad could come back for her but he convinced her to chance it. That day Dad had one of his many accidents. She broke her arm and was badly bruised and hospitalized for a number of days because she didn't have a seat belt in the backseat. No one else was hurt.

I looked at Colin and Jack. Even Colin was shocked by that notion of Mom without a seatbelt. Colin had seen them leave. They had been at his house babysitting just before they left to drive to Riverhead. Colin was sure there was nothing unusual about their departure that would have kept them from repeating their habit to buckle up.

Jack just said "That's crazy." He let the doctor keep talking. She talked about Mom's injuries being mostly to her chest. "She obviously hit the steering wheel," she added.

When we left I said, "It is more than crazy, it has got to be wrong! Think of all the times we have sat in driveways while Mom was digging around in the seats for seatbelts when she was only going a few blocks. It was unimaginable that she would get into her own car, with easy to find seatbelts, and prepare to drive all the way to Riverhead, and not fasten her own seatbelt. And what about the airbag? That car has an airbag! She should not have hit the steering wheel with so much force as to kill her if she had an airbag, even if her seatbelt came unfastened or something." Jack and Colin both calmly agreed.

I could see Jack and Colin knew something more. They had been to the car. They did not think the steering wheel had caused injuries. It was not damaged or distorted by the crash. Steering wheels that kill people are usually warped, or at least noticeably damaged.

Jack had been thinking all along that the air bag had deployed and, because Mom was only five feet tall, and sat very close the steering wheel in order to reach to peddles and to see out, and because the steering wheel was positioned somewhat vertically to allow her to sit close, the air bag deployed right into her chest. I could easily agree with him now.

The Lost Ring

Mom's rings never showed up. Even after the autopsies, we asked the funeral director if Mom was still wearing them. He said she was not. He did share with us his observations. He mentioned that Dad had a very serious looking injury across the back of his neck and shoulder on the right side. That confirmed our picture of Dad wearing his seat belt and shoulder belt and reaching over to take the steering, and thus being out of position.

We searched the house thoroughly for the rings. We thought that perhaps Mom might have been doing some art project that would damage the rings and she took them off and left them with her painting supplies or by the sink. Her rings were always caked with spackle and paint so I was pretty sure that she normally didn't take them off for art work. We even checked the garden shed. I suddenly realized, that her other favorite piece of jewelry was missing also. That was a cameo which she wore a lot. She especially loved it because she bought it when she was grieving for her mother. It was like one

Grandma Munro wore very often that was passed on to an older sister, or perhaps to Aunt Dot. I found that very old one with Mom's things. Her sister must have known it was important to her, and given it to her. But I did not find Mom's own smaller cameo.

We took a trip to New York in July. Tom and I arrived in Greenport before Jack. I checked the answering machine and the first message on the tape was "Mrs. Heitzman, your jewelry piece is ready. Please come in and pick it up." They gave a phone number. Of course! When they borrowed the money on the house she had a little extra, so she had her diamond reset! It makes all the sense in the world. Jack's wedding is coming up. She is thinking about those things especially at this time. I hurried down to the jeweler. Only the cameo mystery was solved. She had that mounted on a chain. She had talked with the jeweler about her plans to attend Jack's wedding, and she wanted that cameo for that. I paid for the new setting, and I sent it to Jack's fiancé. I am sure it was intended for her.

As we began hearing stories about air bag accidents a theme began to recur. The tremendous force of the air bags going off causes hand injuries to drivers. It sometimes blows rings right off of people's hands. In vain we searched the area of the accident and the car.

Air Bags and Other Wind Bags

Jack, having lived his entire adult life in Detroit and having an inside track on automotive rumors had always suspected the air bag. In fact, he believed that a sensor malfunctioned, and the air bag deployed prematurely, not only killing Mom, but causing the accident in the first place. My theory of a heart attack was eliminated. Jack's theory was the only one that still made sense.

Now that I knew what Jack was thinking I was really feeling angry. How is it possible that a company that advertises safety and personal attention, as does the Saturn car manufacturer, allow these beautiful people to lose their lives just by the design of the safety system? How could our government require air bags to be installed in all new cars if they can kill people? Did the testing of the air bag happen during a golf game, or a long lunch? Whatever were they thinking? A car can't go this wrong without someone having an inkling of the possibility. Even the thought of such a thing should have at least triggered a second look. We were looking Satan square in the eye. All I could feel was a wish to lay blame!

I have been to Hell and I met the devil there. In case you are wondering, yes, the devil is a red little goat, with a human mind. He is as red as a warning sticker. He is the very goat the ancient Israelites sent out into the dessert bearing their sins away. He is the scape goat that still carries all the blame. He orchestrates atrocities with his only skill, blame. "Blame the Indians," "blame the Jews," "blame the young people," "blame the old people." The pitch fork is the traditional hand tool for spreading manure. That is what he does by passing blame from one person to the next. Every war, every scar on the human soul bears this stamp of passing the blame often done in the name of God's judgment. He is totally constructed in the human imagination, of nothing but blame.

e-mail From Below

From: The Devil Hisself
              <sssatan@hell.org>

To: Julie <pidgy@enter.com>

Date: July 20, 1997

Subject: Blah, blah, blah

Hi Julie!
I have a little bone to pick with you. After all we have been through together, how can you call me a "construction of nothing but blame?" That would make me fictitious, created only in the mind of the believer. And I assume you think you are real. How can you, a mere insignificant human be real, while I am relegated to being a product of human imagination? I am, of course, the maker of human history! I am the total source of the interesting part of any book, movie, or made for T.V. movie. I am a significant religious figure throughout history. I am real. I am like God. If I am imaginary, then so is God. You radical, liberal, feminists are all the same. You think you have answers, when no one cares about asking the questions.
Please e-mail back right away, it will only prove my point

Yours, Ever, The Devil.

From: Julie <pidgy@enter.com>

To: The Devil Hisself <sssatan@hell.org>

Date: July 20, 1997

Subject: What's Real, What's Not

Hi You Old Devil, You!

That just goes to show that anyone can get an e-mail address.

Let me clear something up right now. I never said you weren't important. Lots of important things are imaginary. Many of the things we human beings regard very highly are created by the human imagination, for example the value of money, and the existence of Santa Claus, to list but two. But that is one significant distinction between God, and you. God is real. God would exist whether or not human beings believed in God. Our prayers do not create God. God is, and was and will be beyond time.

Oh, I've heard your drill. "Can you see, hear, touch, taste, feel God? No you can't prove God is real with even the most modern science. So how can you say, 'God is?'"

And I could give you the traditional answers, Just as surely as Caesar's face was on the old Roman coins, so is God's face on all of Creation. I could tell you to look at the natural beauty all around us, and then you could not say there is no God. You would mumble something about Pantheism, or you might take the "Survival of the fittest" rationale to explain away the magnificence of the Creation. But whose hand beaded the first DNA string?

We sing in a popular spiritual[12], that the whole world is in God's hands. We sing, "The Moon and the Stars are in God's hands." "The little, bitty baby is in God's hands." "You and me sister, are in God's hands." If we, and all that is created are "in God's hands," how then can we "see" God? From this vantage point of the palm of God's hand all we can see are a few whorls of the holy fingerprint. God is too big, and all encompassing for us to distinguish with our mere human senses. We cannot "see" God. If something is beyond perception by the sense of the human face then science cannot declare it as factual.

To use science and senses to find God we would need a control group, so to speak. We know something feels rough to touch because we know what is smooth. We can only identify silence because we have heard sounds. With nothing void of God, we cannot compare non-God with God. Oh, I know you try. Try as you may, even if you were real, you would only be another part of God's creation. You can never be the un-God. You would like to claim a place as the spiritual black hole. But if there was such a thing as a "black hole of the spirit" what would disappear first? You would. Good-bye Devil.

I know God is, because my prayers are answered.

Don't bother to e-mail me back. There is nothing more to say. Bye, bye.

---

[12]"He's Got the Whole World in His Hands" is a traditional spiritual.

Original Grace

Every few hundred years, this idea of original grace emerges as though it is an amazing, all new concept. Really, it is older than time. It is part of God's very nature.

Martin Luther found it deeply entwined throughout Paul's letters to the churches of his wanderings. We are justified by grace alone. Luther took that biblical concept at a time when an alternate system of salvation was being touted. He started a whole genre of bible scholars on a quest after this baffling concept "justification by faith through grace." That is, God rescues peoples' souls because God is gracious, not because people deserve to be rescued.

This idea removes the elements of reward and punishment from God's distribution of blessings. God's grace falls like the rain on the just and the unjust. "Sin equals suffering" is not the equation. In fact, grace also seems to call into question the whole notion of equations. Grace confuses "cause and effect," and on that profane sequence, all of humanly generated science rests. The irony of this is both fascinating and chaotic.

God's grace justifies even sinners. God's grace leaves it up to humanity to do all the blaming. And it also leaves a world of lost souls confused by holy blamelessness. It heaps on our heads coals of God's relentless love. How can we do enough as mere mortal human beings to receive life from a power which is all encompassing love?

Because God is all loving and all powerful, human actions and human curses do not really work to bring punishment from Heaven (or Hell) down (or up) upon the cursed. If that were so, then the mere act of burning witches would have purified the world of evil long ago. If God could be manipulated by human imagination, that is, if cursing worked, then cursing would be an easy explanation for my journey through Hell. The woman in the auto accident wished me off to Hell, amongst the various other words intended to make holy things unholy. But because curses really don't work she must use a lawsuit to bring judgment against me. Think of all the wars and retaliations that could be replaced with cursing if human curses really evoked and manipulated God's response.

When the news of my parent's deaths became known, the letters, that are so hard for our friends to write started pouring into our house. Every letter and card brought me a sense of peace and closeness to caring people. The short "just signed their name" cards said to me "I care about you, but I don't know what to say." The long letters said to me "I care about you, and I have actually thought of something to say." The letters were each little earthly examples of grace. Each word of caring fell like a gentle rain drop, plopping at random on flowers and weeds alike, without judgment, or measure for repayment.

Yet there were some people I did not hear from at all. In retrospect, these may have been the letters I was glad were never written. When I was first diagnosed with cancer I wrote to one particular friend asking for her prayers. Then I shared with her the news about my parents since she had met them in Ohio. She was a macrobiotic diet enthusiast. She not only cared about spiritual things, but also about health things as well. When I wanted to hear from her I was thinking she may have some useful bits of wisdom to impart to me in my time of need. I really felt that my request for prayers would be honored. Somehow I felt like her prayers would really be functional since she was a "health nut." I was sure that carried some weight. But now, as I think what she might have said in that unwritten letter to me, I realize it would have been something about how by living a pure and good life she herself was spared cancer and hardships. She would have taken the role of Job's neighbors. She would have been in search of blame, and since it happened to me, I would be to blame. But by not acknowledging my difficulties, my friend saved me from those Jobian (I know the word for Job-like isn't "Jobial") dialogues in which the righteously un-afflicted ask "what sin have you committed, that God would judge you so harshly?"

Blaming adds a scientific superficial overlay of "cause and effect" to a spiritual journey which in reality can only be guided by grace. The idea that if you find the cause, and you have found the cure blames the patient. It also replaces the mystery of God's grace with a known and earned rescue.

 have often thought that our traditional use of psychoanalysis seems to rely on this perversion of grace by actually equating the cure with "blamability." If you can just remember back to a time when it, whatever "it" is began, you can blame parents or your early childhood, and be done with the problem. When you find that quintessential cause, the problem is cured. Of course, I do have to admit, that blaming actually worked for me. My terror of becoming stainless steel was eased by recalling, and thus blaming, my early acquaintance with stainless steel in the steely cold ambiance of the office of a surgically pure doctor with a colorless metallic persona. Now that I can say that, it can't happen to me. No, wait a minute. I am not free of fear because I found a way to place blame for that fear. I am no longer afraid of doctors with stainless steel tools because I have experienced grace at the hands of doctors. Forgiving my

imagined memoriam to scarey doctors was the source of healing, not blaming.

Perhaps, even for psychiatry, that kind of search for the source and blame approach may be going the way of blood-letting. Healers of social and psychological problems that I have heard lately are teaching the use of "I"[13] statements, like "I feel you are untruthful," as opposed to saying "You're a bald-faced liar." These "I" statements are intended to remove the blame element, and allow for discussion and eventually forgiveness.

Blame or "justice" as it is often euphemistically called, is costly. It obliterates peace and goodwill. It is, of course, the complete antithesis of grace. It is the conspicuous result of original sin, if sin could ever be considered "original" at all. There was no original sin until Paul came along and named it that so that he could explain "original grace" for which he used the word "Christ." All this original sin stuff gets so confusing that it really only sounds sensible when it is explained in some ancient and dead church language.

But the simple little folk story is clear. It's in all the bibles, not just the Christian version.

There were these two "first" people, Adam and Eve. There was a garden which was the assembly of all of God's created blessings. There was a tree of "the knowledge of good and evil." (That knowledge would thus be the ability to cast judgment and i.e. "blame.") The fruit of the tree offered the ability to judge between good and evil was dangerous because

---

[13]One resource explaining "I" statements is: *Alternatives to Violence Workbook* by John Looney from Peace GROWS, Inc. Akron, Ohio. Copyright©1986.

it would make people become like God. In all their primitive wisdom the ancient people passed on this story about the mortal conclusion of human immortality.

If sin was ushered into the world when humankind ate of the tree of the knowledge of good and evil, this dining out also caused embarrassment, hiding, guilt, (those products of judgment and blame) which led to more blame. Adam blamed Eve, Eve blamed the serpent. No one could ever again experience pure grace.

The Fatal Flaw

These days I am reading every morsel of medical news, watching every medical update on the news programs, hoping for something on which we can all blame cancer. If we can blame, we can cure with science.

I am waiting for lawyers to schedule sessions so I can officially get blamed for a car accident I did not feel I had caused. If we can blame we can cure with money.

And now we have another use for blame. We are desperately seeking to blame the deaths of our parents on some one, or some thing. Before I heard about this potential to blame the air bag, it was just something that happened that ended their lives. It protected them from separation from one another. It protected them from the pain of having to face their own aging, and financial woes. It was a big loss for us, but I did not perceive it as an "evil" deed. Then the serpent slithered into the scene again. Blaming stirred a hot-bed of anger in me. The more I thought about it, the more I leveled blame. The more I blamed, the angrier I became.

In the months to come I started clipping news items about air bags. Names of individuals and of groups were emerging who, like us, were questioning the safety of air bags. We learned that there were many people grieving for the dead victims of air bags. There were many more who were injured and were suffering. The stories told of the brutal and random killings of innocent people. Many of the victims were children. In fact, this particular hazzard selected children and short people specifically to be its victims. I guess in the automotive world only tall, young men are valuable. Small sized people, the very young and the old are just spare parts in the collection of the humankind. Had I really accepted this idea I wouldn't have bothered to survive cancer. It all would have been so simple.

At the time Rosie and Milt were shopping for that Saturn I had just bought a used car without an air bag. I mentioned the rumors that air bags were dangerous for short drivers. Mom said they had looked into that. Dad said he checked it out, and all the "experts" were saying air bags are perfectly safe. The official reports said they were safe. "And anyway," Mom added, "they only go off if you crash, and if this car gets wrecked it will probably happen when Milt is driving, and he will be saved by it." I am short. I know not to buy one of these cars. I know this now but after I talked with Mom and Dad about this I thought agreed with her, that the air bag dangers were just rumors.

It took months. When we finally received the autopsies our perception of the crash was confirmed. Mom died of blunt force trauma. She also had bruises across her hips where the seat belt held her, when the car hit the tree. Why did the air bag not protect her from this? We believe it is because it had already gone off. Dad's autopsy confirmed the shoulder belt across his neck and a head bump from the windshield. We believe that was because he was reaching across to take the steering wheel and guide the car.

I heard a statistic that only eighty seven people had been killed by air bags. I called the National Highway Safety Transportation Administration to tell them about Mom and Dad and let them know they needed to add two more to the numbers killed.

The woman who answered the telephone did not even ask, how did I know. She did not seem very interested in correcting this statistic at all. She said the accident would have to be investigated. If we could prove the air bag had caused a death, then we could get it recorded. She also added that if they get a lot of complaints about one particular thing they would then look into that problem.

I asked her if they were getting a lot of complaints about air bag senors going off randomly. She said right now they are not looking at air bags deploying without an accident. They only act when there are lots of complaints. I wondered how many little old women had silently plowed into trees or other cars and had died before they had a chance to place a formal complaint. In the deadly cases, with severe wreckage it is complicated to observe a simple cause, and if the cause was an air bag just going off no one really wants to know.

I asked, how do we proceed with getting an accident investigated so that it will be listed as a "complaint?" It was explained to me that the air bag was designed with "ways to tell" if it went off prematurely. The manufacturer can analyze it. I asked, how can we have that analyzed? She said, we would need to have the automobile manufacturer do the analysis. She gave me the 800 number of the Customer Service Department of the Saturn company. Now my cynicism seemed like sense. I had sense enough to know that if I call the car manufacturer and tell them, "Hey, your car killed my parents" they would not enter into an investigation with an opened mind. I wondered how the statistic of "eighty seven killed" ever got recorded at all. Did all of these people's families hire their own investigators and lawyers, and have lawsuits or something?

If eighty seven people's deaths were reported after long and costly investigations, then how many deaths were not reported because some people are basically either too decent or too poor to go around suing? And what about all the deaths where there were no autopsies or investigation, where the cause was "unknown?"

This death by air bag statistic seems to be only the tip of a large, *Titanic* sinking sort of iceberg. It's that "science above sense" thing again. According the NHSTA, action to

correct dangerous engineering is motivated by statistics, not by actual deaths. So, no matter if your mother or your child is killed, no matter if lots of people are dying, if they are not counted, their deaths really don't count. And counting requires proving that the air bag, above all other possibilities, caused the death. Even when Jack and I have a clear picture of the crash, even when we have gotten autopsies and impounded the car, we cannot have their deaths counted.

As the months went on, I did read about reports of air bags deploying randomly, for no reason. Several models of GM cars were recalled, not including the Saturn. But by this time I knew that GM used the same or similar air bags components in all of its cars. Isn't it odd that the thousands of reported cases of air bags going off at random, with no accident, were in stopped cars, or slow moving cars, so crash deaths were not an issue? Or could it be, that the kind of crash an air bag causes at highway speeds are deadly, but they cannot be sorted out easily. The reason for the crash is unclear because of the damage done in the crash, so it is not listed as "caused by an air bag deploying randomly." Statistically, it did not occur.

How many short women and older people just drove off the road and into a tree? How many of their children said "she was old, it must have been a heart attack." Some of those might belong in the air bag statistics. But they go unrecorded. They literally don't count.

I once believed manufacturers would correct a deadly error as soon as a danger was known. I thought the possibility of one death might be enough to merit a design change. But my parents bought their used Saturn several years after air bag use was required. By this time it was widespread, and well more than one life had already been lost, but not publicized, and the auto manufacturers and all of the major decision makers were simply playing the blame game. Some say it is the manufacturer, some say it is the government who is to blame, for requiring air bags. Maybe people who ride in the cars with the bombs mounted in the steering wheels are to blame. The implications of stories we read said parents of the dead children were to blame for putting their children in the front seat. Short people were to blame for sitting too close to the steering wheel.

The requirement that cars have warning stickers to inform parents of the danger of air bags to children came along after Mom and Dad died. But the campaign to tell parents not to put their children in the front seat could have saved Mom's and Dad's lives even though it was directed at children. Mom probably would never have bought a car with a warning sticker on the safety equipment, even if it was aimed at keeping children's car seats out of the front seat. She knew she was short. She did not go on roller coasters where shortness was a negative factor even though those warning labels were directed to children. But at that time she had no way of knowing that being short was really a factor in air bag safety.

The Real World

Keeping flawed products a secret may appear to be good business in a world where the first rule is, "blame someone else; don't get caught yourself." Sometimes we hear that called the "real world" because the oust from Eden when human beings started judging things "good" and "bad" led people to think reality must be some disgusting state.

"Realistic" drama is costumed with a holey tee-shirt. Poetry for the "real" world is woven with short, four-letter syllables. When the "real" world is simply the mucky underbelly of life, that land beyond Eden where work is drudgery, and childbirth agony, we separate ourselves from the truth that all tee-shirts start out clean and new, our language is multi-syllabic, working is an opportunity for personal accomplishment and fulfillment, and children are a blessing. When we can only perceive reality as a revolting stench we are actually being as unrealistic as the cartoon monkeys who see no evil, hear no evil, speak no evil, and probably wear a clothespin on a nose as well. That is not to say the real world does not stink. It just doesn't stink all of the time in all places.

The real world is the real world. It is neither inherently good nor inherently bad. Yet we have a hard time believing in a reality that is not bad.

As a temp I have worked for lots of companies. Some companies do have a policy, "whatever you do, don't get caught." But not all companies are like that. I sometimes work for a lawn furniture designer. I have seen this small business accept the financial loss for a vendor's error just because the owner/designer wants his product to be good, not because it is killing people, or possibly even likely to.

I answered the telephone one afternoon while the family who owned the business was away. Two of the calls were to thank this family for offering to refinish a particular chair because they did not feel the finish measured up to the company standards. Every caller's voice at that telephone sounded happy to be calling — customers, sales people (of course sales people, they always sound happy) but even the post office people liked calling that place. The owners of this company had a habit of living in a real world which also has a positive side. They were not destroyed by integrity, they were strengthened by it.

Jack and I talked with the lawyer for the estate about finding an investigator to determine the cause of the car crash. The lawyer found an expert investigator in New Mexico who advertised a specialty in air bags accidents. The proposed cost of such an investigation had more zeros after the numeral than I had graph paper boxes in my personal budget. We were astounded. But, we had already committed to such a thing by having the car impounded at a rather high daily rate. So we decided to go ahead and pay the big bucks and get it done right. We felt driven to have the truth interpreted through science, so that we could do something, but we were not sure what. The catch phrase is "get justice."

ustice," as it is commonly used in our legal system is just another product of blame. It seems like a good thing. But just as the blindfolded goddess implies, justice is a balancing act that never is quite even unless nothing is in the scales. It is a constant adjustment to some acceptable facsimile to righteousness we call "fairness." But it never really accomplishes it. Justice never brings peace. Justice, as a bi-product of blame negates forgiveness.

Peace is a result of forgiveness and grace. Grace and blame are not co-inhabitants of the same way of thinking. Justice requires jail sentences. It wins lawsuits. It gives more money to the suffering. Peace offers less need for money, and less suffering. And yet my human nature straight from my original need to blame, straight from my origins in the garden with the serpent left me saying, "Blame someone!"

The Search for Justice

There may be another side to this. There is the belief that justice is an equivalent of peace--a great peace from God. It is how God intended for us to live. That is fine. But the best description of that great peace, or shalom, is the peace that "passes understanding." It is God's justice which equals peace, not just some humanly understandable system of equality. It is beyond our human making. This kind of peace that actually could be equivalent justice comes from God. It is not something we can dictate as human beings no matter how good our lawyers get. God's justice is undoubtably light years past human understanding and is probably something that nurtures life, and exposes love. God's justice is most likely vastly different from the excuse for retaliation human beings label as "justice."

I didn't just think this up. My father knew this truth. Try as he did, he wanted Jack and me to understand it. As children, we did not. We each were always begging our parents for justice through equality. Jack got to go to Grandpa's farm for an extra week, I got to ride on a train. There was no formula to show that we were equal in the sight of our parents. I got a home made dress, and he got shoes when they had money enough to buy us something. Never mind the fact that these things met our needs. I knew the shoes cost more. He knew the dress took more of Mom's time. We complained that we were not treated equally. It was unfair.

Dad presented a challenge for us. He said, "when you come to me with two things that God created, that are the same, I will see that you children are treated exactly the same." I knew there was a trick here, still I jumped at the chance to get justice. So I went on a quest to find two identical things in nature. Of course I knew enough to rule out snowflakes, and fingerprints, and fingerprints, being attached to fingers, implied that no two people are exactly alike. Jack was discussing the matter with some identical twins we knew. I was afraid he would find the answer before I did, and he would achieve true fairness first. He knew about things like chickens and cows that might actually come in duplicates. My experience was with dogs and cats, and wild things. I knew each of those creations was unique. I finally negotiated to use a hypothetical solution. Dad accepted. I said, "how about conjoined twins, seeing their reflection in a still lake?" Even as a nine year old I could see this was flawed. I think Jack seemed convinced that I had won. I think Dad was ready to take any answer just so he could illustrate to us what being treated exactly the same was like.

That night at dinner I found I had a six year old's portion of Jack's favorite foods. I was assured that breakfast would be my usual bowl of cereal. Jack realized he would get the same thing, and he complained. He was an egg and toast guy. I think we only experienced about an hour of actual justice before I admitted there was no equality in nature. Jack was not sure what happened to the conjoined twins beside still water, but I think he was glad to give up justice also. We both received grace randomly from that day on, although I think they loved us both.

"Equality and justice for all" are great edicts for the laws and other such systems created by human beings. But in the real world, God's love, like that of a father or mother, is so much bigger and better than these petty legalistic distribution systems. We can not even venture to know its boundaries.

Jack and I were faced with a decision which put this idea of justice to the test. Should we pursue this investigation of this accident in order to sue, and thus play this worldly sort of justice game, or should we search out the answers and the proof of our premonitions simply to expand the pool of knowledge? We knew one way or the other we were going to have an investigation of the accident done. We both needed to do that. But what to do with the information was the question.

On one hand, a lawsuit would work to translate the deaths of our parents into a monetary figure designed to hurt some guilty and clearly blamable party. (Not to mention the possible windfall that could come our way.) Two human lives are certainly worth a nice piece of ocean front property, and a new sail boat, or even a nice sea plane. This disaster could be rearranged to be my chance at more exotic cancer treatments, and Mariah's college education. Mom and Dad would want these things for us.

On the other hand, what we really know about our parents' understanding of justice is that this notion of "evening a score" or taking an "eye for an eye," which is the intention of punitive damages, only nurtures the most base and profane dimensions of being human. There is nothing holy in that. Winning a court case is an alternative to forgiveness. You can't really both sue, and forgive. Legal battles are the antithesis of the spiritual love that defined the earthly lives and most certainly is the eternal life of our parents. If we didn't hear that in words, we saw their example of it repeatedly.

When I was a senior in high school, a week before the prom, I was practicing on the apparatus in gym class. I fell from the parallel bars and was knocked unconscious. Most of my teeth were cracked or broken and I had a stitched up chin for the prom. A few weeks later some men in suits appeared at our door all powered up in their most intimidating shades of navy and dark grey. My high school had sent them to either make a deal, or to do battle with the parents of "the victim." That was what they called me. I listened from the top of the stairs. My parents invited them in and served them coffee and brownies.

The visitors started by assuring my parents that a thorough investigation was under way and the gym teacher who failed to place the mats under the apparatus would be punished by losing her job. They also said that they would talk with our lawyers about a fair monetary settlement. If we insisted on suing, however, they were prepared to fight.

My dad called me down to sit in on the meeting. I listened as he explained that he would do whatever he could to help the teacher keep her job. He said that since it happened at school, the school accident insurance was covering my immediate medical bills. There was no financial need. The important thing, he explained, was that no one would have their lives ruined by this simple mistake. The Long Island lawyers were confused. They had lost their edge. Now, they were expected to eat Mom's homemade brownies graciously. They didn't know how to do that very well. It was a treasured, awkward lawyer moment. They left without even a routine "thank you." The next day Dad called the school. He argued that we did not want the gym teacher's life to be ruined just because of one human mistake.

I don't know that the school, or the teacher or the lawyers felt good about the outcome. But I know there is a good feeling that comes to the person who offers forgiveness. To this day, whenever I go get more fillings in my teeth I think of that gym class accident, and about the clean, free feeling that comes from practicing forgiveness. It feels good not to live as the "sue-er." And we are quite sure that Mom and Dad would not want their heirs to be wealthy from a lawsuit on their behalf.

Forgiveness is Lost in the Shuffle

Our parents were vulnerable to crimes. These two people in their seventies rarely locked their doors. They lived in a neighborhood with various racial groups and various economic circumstances. They lived only a block from the ending of the Long Island Railroad and the port for the Shelter

Island Ferry. Strangers passed by their house regularly. My dad befriended people with various needs because he felt it was his spiritual calling. He was always breaking the safety rules by picking up hitchhikers, or stopping to help some poor drunk get safely to his destination. Yet Mom and Dad were never mugged or beaten or robbed at gunpoint.

Thoughts of their vulnerability often haunted me though. As I pictured them in danger, I also imagined them saved by the same loving, gentle nature that left them vulnerable. Their constant, unwavering message was forgiveness. Dad's favorite passage for a sermon topic was from 1st John chapter 4, vs. 18.

> "There is no fear in love; perfect love drives out all fear. So then, love has not been made perfect in anyone who is afraid, because fear has to do with punishment."[14]

I know that if a gun was put to their heads they would be fearless. They would be thinking of the human motives of the murderer. They would offer food and share what they had. They would offer forgiveness, and tell this person that he or she did not have to be afraid. They would make their last words a refuge from the fear and greed that motivated the killing.

All of us, who are their family, would follow the investigation. We would applaud an arrest. We would attend the trial. We would listen to the murderer, and we would try to understand what human reason this person could have to take the lives of these two beautiful people. Is this person needy, and a robber? Is this person simply greedy? Is this person

---

[14]*Today's English Version* — Second Edition
© 1992 by American Bible Society. Used by Permission.

crazy, or heartless? Is this person just someone fascinated with the machinery of weapons?

Now, as it happened, we do believe that they were killed because of some sort of fear or greed. Maybe the NHSTA (that's the National Highway Safety Transportation Administration.) was afraid of letting the dangers of air bags be known, after it had supported the mandatory use of air bags. Maybe the auto makers were just greedy and cut corners in the air bag design.

When a big corporation kills its own customers because of greed, it is no different than when a mugger on the street pulls out a gun and shoots his victims, as he robs them. The motive is the same, greed. The result is the same, death. The difference is, there is no one to look in the eyes, and say, "I forgive you." There is a corporate logo and an advertising campaign. There is an office building and a factory. There are groups of nameless, faceless employees, working for their paychecks. But there is no human face on this greedy murderer. There is no one to forgive.

There is an empty space. Without forgiveness there is no ending, no healing...

I wanted to find a person to blame, if not for the sake of blaming, then at least to offer forgiveness. I clipped news articles, and searched the Internet, and collected as much material about air bags as I could find. I read over the stacks of papers for research into the engineering and testing of various air bag components. I scoured the material to find a name and a face. There were so many parts, and so many tests, and so many little decisions. It was not as simple as answering "Who invented the electric light?" We all know that was Edison, or was it.... Benjamin Franklin?

I decided to limit my search to who invented the air bag sensor? That was the part that probably failed first. Then I found the answer. I know some great invisible angel of forgiveness was sitting with me, flipping the pages of the large collection of material, driving my focus to the design of the sensor. First I read about tests at Wright Patterson Air Force Base. "Hey, that's only twenty minutes from our old home and church in Kettering, Ohio." That is where we lived for a decade before we moved to Pennsylvania. Then, I looked at the next page. The sensors that were possibly used by General Motors (Saturn) were designed by engineers by the Delco Company. To my ears "Delco" was not a brand name on a faceless product. It was the name of the neighborhood park where we went with our friends to hear music and watch fireworks. It was the green space near the church. It was the employer of our friends and the people who made up the church.

In my mind's eye, suddenly, the engineers had names and faces. I knew them. They were with the people who argued to keep music and the arts in the school system. They were with the people who started a group to discuss ways we could be active in the world to make peace and alleviate hunger. They were good, and clear thinking people. We had shared food and prayers and tears. We had sung songs together and gone on retreats. They were my friends.

I know them, and I think I can understand their motives. They were trying to save people. Maybe it's like the chef who creates a fabulous potato salad, only to have it left in the sun while the wedding pictures are being taken. Something created for goodness sake becomes deadly. If I sort through each component in the creation of the air bag I will see only more people who had only the best of intentions. Who is to blame? Who is to forgive?

Perhaps the real irony is this. The only actual function of an air bag is to save lives. It was not designed to be tasty or nutritious, or to enhance the appearance or the function of the car. It is just for safety. That is all. It is like a gun in the cash drawer. No one really likes it. It could easily kill an innocent person. The big difference is, a gun is known to be dangerous. It is optional, and in fact, discouraged by laws in favor of keeping people alive. The explosive device in the steering wheel of newer cars is not optional. Even after it has killed a large number of people, it is now required. It is not just one of many choices on the buffet table. It is the only way cars come. I am sure my friends who worked for Delco, and people I know who work on testing at Wright Pat, were designing sensors to be marketed, and thus "chosen" by the consumer. Each engineer along the way was simply creating one of many choices.

But somewhere along in the process of research and design, science and creation, this so called "safety device" was sucked into the mysterious, smoking pits of Hell where ignorance is bliss. Actual information was edited for market. Catch phrases replaced actual useful information. "Air bags save more lives than they take" was the tag ending of nearly every story about air bag dangers, whether it was on the news or in the publications put out by the NHSTA.

In the pamphlet entitled *Air Bags & On-Off Switches Information for an informed Decision — Keeping the Benefits for the Many and Reducing the Risks for the Few* This NHSTA pamphlet breezes over the potential for death by using these manipulated statistics.

Air bags are proven, effective safety devices. From their introduction in the late 1980's through November 1, 1997, air bags saved about 2,620 people. The number of people saved increases each year as air bags become more common on America's roads.

However, the number of lives saved is not the whole story. Air bags are particularly effective in preventing life-threatening and debilitating head and chest injuries. A study of real-world crashes conducted by the National Highway Traffic Safety Administration (NHTSA) found that the combination of seat belts and air bags is 75 percent effective in preventing serious head injuries and 66 percent effective in preventing serious chest injuries. That means 75 of every 100 people who would have suffered a serious head injury in a crash, and 66 out of 100 people who would have suffered chest injuries, were spared that fate because they wore seat belts and had air bags.

For some people, these life saving and injury-preventing benefits come at the cost of a less severe injury caused by the air bag itself. Most air bag injuries are minor cuts, bruises, or abrasions and are far less serious than the skull fractures and brain injuries that air bags prevent. However, 87 people have been killed by air bags as of November 1, 1997. These deaths are tragic, but rare events --" [15]

---

[15]*Air Bags & On-Off Switches Information for an informed Decision — Keeping the Benefits for the Many and Reducing the Risks for the Few* U.S. Department of Transportation, National Highway Traffic Safety Administration, DOT HS 808629.

"Air bags save more lives than they take." I certainly don't question the truth of that at all, just the common sense behind it. What kind of safety device is it that is touted as simply saving more people than it kills? Would you buy a life-jacket if the best truthful sales pitch was that it saves more people than it kills? Would you buy a car seat for a baby if the ad simply said it saves more babies than it kills? I am sure my parents would not have bought the used car with the optional air bag if any official person, be it the NHSTA, GM, Saturn, or anyone would have told them they kill children and short people.

Jack and I have plotted our wild wish for a resolution to this. I would like to go to the executive conference rooms of NHSTA, GM, and Saturn and place two permanently empty chairs at these important conference tables to memorialize the earthly lives of Milt and Rosie Heitzman, innocent victims of the choices made at these conference tables. Then, when the living people at the table call in the corporate lawyers to weigh the financial cost of lawsuits against the cost of correcting a flawed product, these empty chairs would gape at them. More chairs would have to be brought in to accommodate the lawyers because these two chairs would remain empty.

The conversation might go, "so, how much is a short driver worth, a million dollars, or maybe two dollars and fifty cents? Who knows? A Cadillac driver is certainly worth more than a Saturn driver because he is more likely to pay for a long-winded lawsuit. A young person is worth more than an old person. There is more earning potential there. A future is worth more than current life. "

I can imagine that the engineers and marketing executives, all those gathered at the table, would see these empty chairs and would be reminded that in the filled chairs around this table are living, breathing human beings, created by God. Like Milt and Rosie had been, they themselves are sacred, holy beings, gifted with life. They are not just empty constructs of money and power -- the prize of a won competition. These decision makers are human beings empowered with choices. They have the power of Cain, to kill their own siblings, or the power of actual greatness to choose life.

CHAPTER 6

Then, Radiation

adiation is part of the initial plan for chasing my cancer. It is the follow-up for surgery that was put on hold while I had chemo. When I first heard the plan, waiting with the radiation seemed like a good idea. I liked the idea of radiation the least of all possible treatments. In fact I often wondered if radiation wasn't actually the culprit in this whole thing. Cancer rates rose steadily since radiation was taken out of the earth and incorporated into weapons and energy sources. But also, my cousin Gwen and I had a brush with this monster when we were in our late teens. I felt that this may have been the cause of our cancers.

Gwen, her brothers and sister, Jack and I, and our other cousins, all got together most summers at Duneswood. As teens, Gwen and I saw ourselves as lifelong best friends. We dreamed our dreams together. We dreamed our dreams of college, and shared our dreams of our futures. We passed fashion magazines back and forth while we tanned on the beach, and talked about wardrobe accessories we could make that would look like the things everyone would be wearing that year. We were both "preacher's kids," ("P.K.'s") and school shopping was usually limited to a pair of new shoes, if we needed them. We shared our common P.K. experiences that flavored the other ten months of each year but did not matter at Duneswood. We took many long walks on the beach talking about these kinds of things, and about more important things as well.

One summer a new shape appeared on the horizon where the beach and the water came together about ten miles to the north. A big, white ball was jutting into the water. We were told it was the nuclear power plant at South Haven. That same year the water temperature went up, causing a huge over population of alewives, a little silver fish. Huge bunches of these dead fish washed onto the shore causing a "national disaster" and the National Guard was called in. They came with tanks, and ran over all the dead fish, and pushed them down into the sand, and fixed the disaster as only men with tanks can do. For some reason, also, that year the sea gulls were no longer in the sky. There were a lot of the them dead on the shore though. It was very sad.

Gwen was undaunted in her plan to have her personal fitness program continue. She had an inborn obstinance. I don't know whether to attribute to the Germans or the Scots in our heritage. This perseverance was coupled with her amazing mind and immeasurable ambition. When she decided to accomplish something, it was done. In spite of the dead things on the beach her plan was to swim two miles and then run two miles. Sometimes one of our mothers' cousins went with her, but when she could find no other long distance swimmer, I walked along on the shore while she swam, and then jogged back with her. I always thought that perhaps we were going too near the radiation when we had gone those two miles up the beach. But everyone said, nonsense, it's got to be safe or "they" wouldn't allow it. As the years passed I have learned that the voice of the "they" isn't always the unanimous truth. It is really just a depository for blame. So Gwen swam, and we ran back, again and again that summer.

I asked Dr. Tallhouse about this radiation experience as a possible cause for our cancers. He assured me that it was long ago and far away, and the cancers caused by radiation happen sooner than either Gwen or I had experienced. It still left me with a very skeptical opinion of radiation. The good thing was that Dr. Tallhouse was the radiation doctor, and he is not confusing or secretive in order to keep me ignorant, thus "positive" or blissful as in the adage "ignorance is..."

I shared with Dr. Tallhouse my concern that my CA27-29 test had gone up to 40, and I did not yet know the results from the test taken at the time of my last chemo treatment. I suggested that I should possibly get a cat, because I am allergic to cats, and when I was having the drug to which I was allergic, my tumor marker number went down. He said he wasn't sure what that had to do with it. I suggested that an allergy is related to one's immune system. And since I have had cancer I have never had a sniffle or any other symptom of anything. So perhaps if I could make my immune system work harder, I would have better luck. This is the point in the conversation with doctors that I expect they write the word "WACK-O" across my chart and stop listening. But Dr. Tallhouse, who was wearing a Tabasco Sauce tie, said, "You mean your auto-immune system... Hummm. Before you try anything as drastic as getting a cat, let's see what the last test results were. I will let you know when they are available." The next morning at 7:30 he called me with those results. It was 37, considered to be "normal." I did not buy a cat, but I started planning my life again.

July, 1997

Radiation begins with simulation. That was the strangest of all medical procedures. I have no vague idea of any scientific accomplishment it could possibly have.

Simulation has a special room and special equipment. A specialized nurse explains that I cannot move a muscle until they are done. So I stripped down, and lay flat and still -- just like a stainless steel table. And like a table, the doctor and nurses walking back and forth around the room, would, from time to time, set things on it. As they got into the project they used the table to prepare various art projects. There was a paper-mache project, in which they made a three dimensional facsimile of my breast. And, there seemed to be lots of drawings done with markers. Then there was photography. Every medium in art figures into this project. For a whole hour and 15 minutes I didn't move a muscle. Lights flashed. People talked as though I was nothing but a table. They needled me. They added tatoos. All of my fears of being taken for a piece of medical equipment, plus my father's fear of radiation and tatoos, were all heaped together here. But since I felt I had the option to move and become human again at any time, this was not the least bit scary. In the end, I had 10 dot tatoos, and lots of gridwork written all over my chest. The doctor and nurses had every dot and line precisely measured, photographed and x-rayed. My personal uniqueness, my odd shaped breast, the location of my lungs and heart and lymphnodes were all accounted for and graphed.

After all this, I put on my $7.98 discount store bra, and realized the gridwork drawn on my skin precisely outlined the bra. Next time I say, leave the bra on, and trace it. It could all be done in five minutes with a Sharpie marker and the right bargain bra.

There is a line between fear and adventure like the center line in a road. It barely separates safe travel from on-coming crashes. It is named "courage." Bertold Brecht reminds us that its spawn is a bunch of undesirable idiots in his grueling musical "Mother Courage and All Her Children." Yet I trust that narrow line to allow me to move forward. Facing the inevitable is no accomplishment in courage. It is going to be faced, courage or not. That is what inevitable means.

Moving forward when it is a matter of choice is the pre-requisite for courage. I really find it annoying to have good intentioned people telling me I have amazing courage, simply because I have cancer. Having cancer does not make someone courageous. I have no choice. Choosing courage makes someone courageous.

People of courage pop up in the most unexpected places. A retired woman who moved here from another state is one example. Irene and I went to lunch to talk about encounters with breast cancer which we had in common. As we visited, I realized this woman has made a whole lifetime of choices. She was always taking the path that required the most courage. She and her sister left their homeland in England to live in a distant city. When she retired from her job she found a nice remote little piece of rural Pennsylvania. There she built a house, and also a whole network of friends in a long established Pennsylvania German community where new people and certainly English people with an English accent, are something of an oddity. She said she came here just by getting in her car and driving down unfamiliar roads. And that is exactly how she found her courage as well. She just went to new places.

I had been continually feeling frustrated by my unfamiliarity with the winding rural Pennsylvania roadways. With several recent reminders that driving a car is a life and death event, my need to drive to the hospital every morning for radiation treatment was looming before me like a dark cloud. The hospital was a little more than a half hour away. That was a whole hour of watching out for hazzards every day. I felt that if I could just become familiar with each road, I would never be surprised while driving along. Therefore, getting from one place to another would be much less stressful. It seemed that choosing the same road, the biggest easiest road, would be the best. And I then I thought of Irene, always making choices for the greatest challenge to her courage. She came to this place because the roads were winding and rural. People of courage consistently choose the most unfamiliar path, whether it is climbing Mt. Everest, or jumping from a plane with nothing but a parachute, or going to a social event with a bunch of strangers. Since I felt what I needed was more courage, I made a conscious effort to look for the new and unexpected.

Quickly my need for more courage in driving vanished. I started seeing things that weren't even hazzards in the roadway, like deer grazing in the dewy fields, and seven huge wild turkeys all trying to perch in the same little leafless sapling. Like another gift from heaven, I found a most beautiful road, that crisscrosses a reservoir on bridges. The spectacular daily sunrises across the water, and the subtle changes from one day

to the next left me feeling, not only less stress, but an underlying sense of joy. It flavored my days, and made me long for the next drive into the sunrise.

Radiation involved daily trips back to the hospital, a wait in a waiting room where everyone wears hospital gowns, and about fifteen or twenty minutes of laying perfectly still, while watching the nurses shifting the heavy equipment all around me. They invited me to bring my own taped music to hear, and the whole thing, for me, was quite painless. So I now rank this as my preference for traditional cancer treatment. Of course I am still holding out for the less traditional methods like aroma therapy, garlic, and a sense of humor.

Sept., 1997

A Letter Home

I have found that writing not only saves my friends and family from having to hear me ramble on, telling my stories, but it also gives me a way to fill in those gaps in my days and weeks that were always spent on the telephone with Mom and Dad. I can write them letters, even though there is no earthly mailing address.

Dear Mom and Dad,
A few weeks ago I dreamed we were riding in my car. I was driving— nothing against your driving intended here, it's just how it was. We were traveling along Route 663 from Pottstown down into our boroughs here in Pennsylvania, and as we crested the hill at the Strawberry restaurant it was twilight or dawn. Suddenly we went from the deep, dark, peaceful woods to this brink of population. Spread out before us were the lights of the towns in the valley. The New Goshenhoppen Church steeple punctuated the busy moving lines of cars' lights. Just as I started down the hill toward home, you vanished from my car, and I realized I must go back alone. I must awaken to the truth that you have both died, not to be with us in life, again, except in my dreams, and in my spiritual journeys.

You are not lost though. I promise you, if a band of angels comes to me, I will look for the only angel in heaven wearing wedding rings. Then I will find you both together there.

These days I can feel you near. I know your joy in living is incomplete. You were not finished with all the neat creative things you had to do. On the day after that dream of you in my car, a very dear friend of yours from Orient called me. (I edited her name out, when this letter was opened for sharing, as I don't think she was one of the "far out" friends who accepted the metaphysical as openly as Mom did. But you know who I mean.) She called to say she had a dream that you were together visiting with her, and she just wanted to share the warm feeling with me.

So, I decided to write to add that earthly dimension of real conversation to our silent meetings, and also, to help me focus my thoughts.

Although the news of your deaths caused the chemotherapy to falter, I am now done with chemo, and with radiation. My tests are coming back suspense fully high, but not so high that I need further treatment at this time.

Dad, now that I have been through it, radiation is a "piece of cake." You would have done fine with it. When we last talked on the phone, the night before your accident, we talked about cancer treatments, and what doctors don't tell you. I asserted my "ask them anyway" philosophy. If you only had time to hear your doctor's answers you would have learned what we know now. Your cancer was confined to the area marked for radiation. You probably would be planning to celebrate the New Year, 1998, as I am, as a time of promise and life, renewed.

Jack and Liz had a beautiful wedding. Mariah and I flew out there, and I rented a car. Tom had too many commitments with the church in September to get away. So I did the Detroit driving. I never realized what a limitation shortness is in driving, since I've always chosen foreign designed cars and German and Japanese people must come in shorter versions than the standard American cowboy, around which American cars are designed. When you go to Detroit, though, you can't rent a Volkswagen or a Toyota. In order to see over the dashboard at the same time my feet were on the peddles I had to get the tiniest little thing that was like tin foil around a flower pot. It was very pretty but it felt like a "just pretend" car. I can see why Mom picked out the Saturn. For a small car, at least, it feels substantial.

I know you were planning to be at this wedding all the way back in May. Your "mother of the groom" dress was half made in a bag in the sewing room, and your little cameo was being reset at the jewelers. Did you mean to give that to Liz? I thought you might, so I made sure she got it.

The ceremony was Polish Catholic. It was at a huge church near Algonac. The men in the wedding party all wore charcoal gray tophats and tails. Jack looked dashing with his dark hair, and gray sideburns. I was so pleased my hair was finally coming back that I did not wear a hat or a wig. Now looking back at the pictures, I see that I did not have as much hair as I imagined. Jack had more, and he got his hair cut for the event. Liz, of course was a totally gorgeous bride. She was the beautiful blonde bride every little girl imagines herself to be on her wedding day.

Mariah and I were among the first to arrive, so we sat on the "Groom's side." Just the two of us, on a whole side of a big sanctuary. Liz has lots of brothers and sisters, nieces and nephews so the whole first section of the bride's side filled up. They kept looking over at me and Mariah, and we kept looking back. I was sure they were gawking at my hair. Dad, I know you would have eased us all through this. We missed your gregarious personality. Finally a sister of Liz's was designated to come over and bring me a corsage which matched the corsage for the mother of the bride. I knew I was representing you. But you would not have been so conspicuously hairless. When we spoke I realized that the awkward barrier keeping our families distant was not my looks, but that Liz's family does not easily speak English. Liz, the youngest child of this large Polish family is the only person in her family who was born in this country.

When the wedding march began, we stood and turned and I saw that Jack had lots and lots of friends there, so the "groom side," only had a shortage in the family part.

Most of the service was in Polish. You know, as long as Jack has lived in the Detroit area the only Polish he speaks is names for sausage. So I was glad their vows were at least in English, so he sort of knows what he is getting into.

The most touching thing for me, and clearly, if you were there, your special moment as well, was Liz's surprise way of bridging the cultural gap, and making our family feel a part of things. After the pronouncement, Jack and Liz faced the congregation as a bag piper came marching down the aisle with that haunting sound penetrating earth and heaven. Jack and I and Mariah were the only ones there who recognized the red and yellow plaid the piper wore as that of the Munro's. I could hardly see it through the tears. It was really a loving tribute to our family's heritage. I know Liz had to jump hurdles for the very traditional Polish priest to allow the three of us that simple statement of belonging. You must have heard the music.

Well, I sure enjoyed this opportunity to share this with you. Let's keep in touch.

Love, Julie

May 1998

Norm

The first move of our married life, after we had acquired a few things to move, was from the married students' apartments to a small town in Ohio, where Tom had his first church.

Being a United Methodist school, most of the changes which caused students to move into parsonages happened in June after the United Methodist Conference assignments. But we are not Methodists. The process of being "called" to a church often takes longer in the denomination to which we belong. As a result, we helped load trucks, and we waved good-bye to all of our friends, one after another, before it was our turn to move. We learned a lot about how not to move. If your congregation is rural, and it is June, consider the possibility that any truck large enough to hold furniture is also the best truck for taking sheep to be sheared or to market. June seems to be the time when sheep ride in trucks a lot. And, the best day to move the pastor is apparently the day after the sheep journeys are completed. So, after watching our neighbors load their households into not so clean livestock trucks, we prepared to be moved by stacking the dirty or most water proof stuff on the bottom. But as luck would have it, our church was in a very tidy little community that took pride in its clean and polished style. It was there I learned that your house isn't clean if you haven't scrubbed the sidewalk. Instead of a large, dirty farm truck, a caravan of just washed pick-up trucks with covered truck beds, (in case of rain) lined up in the seminary parking lot, to move our boxes of books, and our recently acquired chair.

What we learned from that, was that sometimes the volunteers of a church do a better job than the paid pros. And furthermore, it is a great opportunity to meet the real workers of the church one on one, with everyone in work clothes. So the next two times we moved when we were given the choice of hiring a professional mover or having church volunteers do it, we have opted for the chance to save money, and get acquainted instead of hiring the professionals who carry breakage insurance. We have never had to deal with sheep dung or have we ever wished we had our things insured.

About thirty people gathered to help unload the truck that the church sent out to Ohio for us when we came to Pennsylvania. It was a hot, dry, August day, and we actually had filled an entire semi with stuff that accumulated over the years. Our ten original boxes of books had evidently been breeding. Now we had about forty boxes of books. Our one chair had developed lots of siblings as well. So even for thirty people, it was a lot of hard work.

I tried to learn names and faces, and I tried to invent memorizing gimmicks to make what I was learning stick in my memory. For the most part, the women were all named "Mary." Or so it seemed. You would think that would make it easy to remember, but it really didn't. Just one "Betty" confuses the whole thing.

One man with a radiant smile, and a very sharp sense for the engineering that went into moving, wore a name tag, "Norm." He was both frail and energetic. He was clearly a patriarch, but he sort of applied himself in the role of a servant. As I noted these paradoxes, I used the memory device, "Norm" is not the "Norm." He is most unique.

The months passed, and my name learning expanded into actually getting to know a few people better. Norm was constantly involved with church activities. He was always busy helping at Vacation Bible School, or church dinners or wherever the families of the church were gathered. We learned that he was indeed one of the pillars of this community. He had worked for many years in a successful business which he had started.

We were surprised to learn that for nearly two decades he had waged a battle against leukemia. From time to time in the few years we knew him, his health would wane. Then a few days later, we would see him out walking, or mowing, or working in his yard, just as vibrant as ever. He claimed his years of grace were the result of faith in God, and of knowing the truth, even about a life threatening illness like leukemia. His contagious positive attitude lingers with everyone who knew him.

When I was feeling sorry for myself, the "poor cancer victim," I saw Norm at the Strawberry Festival scooping and serving ice cream, enjoying watching all the people coming and going, simply savoring life. I mentioned my experience with the world of medicine. He shared with me his own amazement at the simplicity of it all. Doctors are just people. They don't understand the power of faith, and the possibility that the patient has a brain. A patient can know what is going on. We joked about that. Actually, it was a life thread, not a joke. Norm said that after he lived that first year beyond what the doctors expected, he figured, just do everything to stay healthy and appreciate every day. And that's what he was doing. Now it has been sixteen years of living beyond the limit doctors originally set for him.

But this time now that I am thinking of Norm, and making mental notes for my journal, I am in this church. His grandchildren are reading the poems and eulogies for him. It is Norm's funeral service. We are celebrating a life that was a valuable gift. How much he loved these grandchildren, and how grateful he was for his time to know them. It is another May, and heaven is richer.

I know Norm imagined that cancer could be cured in his lifetime. I still believe that it can happen in my lifetime.

The Cure

I had the CA27-29 blood test periodically as the months passed. For a long time it was in the normal range. Then it went back up to the forties. When I called Dr. Apple's office for those test results the receptionist said "there was no test." So I knew that they must be high, or she would say "The nurse will call you right back and tell you." I was getting to know the routine. I said, please check, I know the test was done. I called back, and she said it was listed as "normal" the last time I'd had the test — not to worry. I asked for a number, and she would not give me a number. Why would she not give me the number? I was sure it was high then. I asked when I could call back and get the number from the nurse. I had to wait four days before she came in to work again. I waited, and just as I thought, the number was forty-one (thirty-seven was the high end of normal.) Forty-two was the highest it had ever been. That was before I had any surgery or treatment or anything.

At my next appointment with Dr. Apple I was determined to tell him of my frustration with getting no bad news from his office. Before my appointment I rehearsed my angry tirade. I was prepared to say, "I need to know test results when I call, because I call when I am prepared to deal with results, when I have time for a walk alone, when I can have some prayer time alone! I do not want visits to the doctor to be made more terrifying by having all these people know things about me that I do not know, then to find out results just as I am getting weighed, and getting my blood pressure checked. I have to come in to the doctor visit 'pre-prayed.' --with no surprises." I really liked that punny little word that had come to me, "pre-prayed." I practiced, "I like to come pre-prayed." It sounded so witty. "I like to come pre-prayed."

But before I could try out the little catch phrases, Dr. Apple's office called. Due to an unforseen circumstance, Dr. Apple would have to reschedule my appointment and I would have to call back another day to know when he would be seeing patients again. It all sounded so impersonal I really didn't ask the human questions in my mind, "What has happened to Dr. Apple?" Instead, I said, that there are some concerns I have now. Is there someone with whom I can talk? She said you might see if you can get an appointment with Dr. Sorroco. She gave me her number. I called her immediately and made an appointment.

Perhaps it was simply a matter of gender. I don't like to see myself as that narrow minded. But having a doctor who has breasts when the subject is breast cancer was very important to me. I had been trying to convince myself that any medical person would do. I don't expect a veterinarian to be a collie or a goldfish. Why should I expect to have a doctor who is of my same physical construct? But a doctor with breasts must have all the fears and wonders that go along with that. I imagine that a woman (even a woman doctor) could find a lump and experience that feeling of wanting to know what this means. I could imagine a woman doctor having mammograms, and P.M.S. And, not only was Dr. Sorroco a woman, I also knew her to be caring. I also knew that she might even confirm her medical knowledge by reading the manuals. I had seen her at the hospital reading manuals.

The media had been full of talk about curing cancer. Perhaps the drug companies just needed to show they were continuing to work. Maybe the cigarette companies or asbestos makers were behind all this hype, trying to present cancer as no longer life-threatening. I don't know what motivated the media to talk about this so much when there wasn't much to say. But they did. I listened carefully to each story. I imagined that others like Norm, who were dealing with the disease in a life and death struggle, listened to the teasers on the news programs, and for a brief moment imagined waking up on a day without cancer. Then the news story came on. "Scientists announced that they are beginning tests on a new drug." "Beginning tests" is a far cry from finding a cure. The only qualified recipients of the new drugs are rats. It's those rats again. First they brought us the bubonic plague. Now they get the good cancer drugs, while people wait in line. It may be years before science can advance the cause to the point of giving the medicine to people.

There was a real news story also about a breast cancer drug that was being tested on people. Since it was very limited to helping only a fraction of breast cancer patients, those with an aggressive type of advanced cancer, it did not get all of the hype in the news the other drug was getting. This drug wasn't on the market yet either. I suppose it was a lot less interesting to talk about since it only applied to those with the inherited type of breast cancer in which there is a "Her II" gene present. (I remember that scientific word, because it is not all that scientific to say, "Her too?") With this, herceptin, a chemotherapy drug can be guided to affect just the cancerous cells, and thus the side affects of chemo can be reduced. This drug and also the stem cell transplant were two treatments that they announced may be available as soon as September of 1998.

Armed with my notepad of details I went to my appointment with Dr. Sorroco ready to share how great it was to have all these new options soon available when and if I need more treatment. Dr. Sorroco was outraged! She said it was totally irresponsible of the few people who claimed to be scientists to report a cure when they had no cure! She said, the "cure" they talk about is years away! It gives people "false hopes."

I could certainly understand what she was saying. She had probably had a string of patients for weeks, living day by day, nearer and nearer to death, wondering why they couldn't take the place of the rats in the experiment, just giving up on the fight for life altogether when they learned the cure was a "false hope." She probably knew these victims of false hopes personally, and she cared for them. So I wonder, are false hopes not better than no hope at all? Then, I sort of think that all hope is false hope, or else, why call it hope? If it was likely to work it would be beyond hope, it would be an "assurance," or a "plan," or an "expectation." The word "hope" seems simply a euphemism for hopeless.

I knew Dr. Sorroco was reacting to that widely publicized rat study. So I asked her more specifically, would I qualify for hercepten if I needed more treatment? Again she said that was a matter of questionable ethics. Women were chosen for the drug trials by lottery. So many women have applied to be a part of the study that they are not taking everyone. You are chosen to get the life giving drug purely by the luck of the draw. People who could be saved, may be dying, just because they did not win this lottery. The lottery system did seem unfair. But it did not pertain to me, since I could not afford to pay for experimental drugs not covered by insurance, not with Mariah preparing for college, anyway. I clarified my concern. "What if I stay healthy until it is through the testing phase, and on the market? Then would I qualify for it?" Dr. Sorroco said my tumor was not tested for the Her II Gene. But in the future, it could be. I was more than hopeful, I was actually planning, and full of expectation, beyond hope.

CHAPTER 7

"Choose Life"

y art teacher in college said "the secret of creating a work of art is knowing when it is finished." I am not sure if that is true for painting, but it is an obvious truth when it comes to recording ones personal journal. As sure as taxes and death, is the fact that this mortal life is a tragedy. We all know how it will end. Yet the true unfolding of the story is that life is a patchwork of experiences. So I look at this checkerboard of eighteen months in my life, and I see that I have changed in ways I never could have predicted. I have a different way of valuing life, and of facing my own mortality.

A few years ago I was a counselor on a junior high youth outing. The other adult leader had planned the event for a beautiful Sunday afternoon in April. We were going on a nature hike with cameras to photograph Spring unfolding. Our pictures would become a display on the church's youth bulletin board. Because the weather was so fabulous, and it was the first such day after a hard winter, and because hiking trails were limited in the suburbs, the great outdoors was not so great. It was crowded with other people. The flower shoots were trampled, and the animals were all in hiding.

As we realized our nature bulletin board would be pretty bleak, we walked along the roadway back to the parking area, when someone suddenly had an idea. We would photograph road kill and other such trash, and make a bittersweet message for our photo display. The small group of junior high boys on this hike thought that was a great idea. They gathered around an opossum corpse, and snapped their cameras. Then they went on to a dead racoon. They thought that was a real find. A bird, and a squirrel also had photo ops. I didn't snap any of these pictures, myself, neither did the girls who were along. We kind of allowed for a gender gap. Personally, I thought it was a creepy idea. But when pictures came back and they were all assembled and mounted, I was surprised.

The series of road kill photos turned out to have a poignant statement to make about death. Some of the animals curled up as if they were sleeping peacefully, and others clearly did not go gentle . They were frozen in time raging into that good night.

The teachers of the ancient law heard God speaking such words.

" I am now giving you the choice between life and death, between God's blessing and God's curse, and I call heaven and earth to witness the choice you make. Choose life."[16]

This passage has a special significance for those of us who read the Genesis story of Adam and Eve as a story in which the eternal damnation was caused by taking the bite of the fruit of the tree of the knowledge of good and evil. When human beings go around applying little human judgments of goodness and badness on everything from child birth to the work ethic, lots of things that are just part of the processes of nature get labeled evil. If people do not find them comfortable, they are evil. Judging the goodness and badness of things seems

---

[16] Deuteronomy 30:19, *Today's English Version* — Second Edition © 1992 by American Bible Society. Used by Permission.

to be the bad thing to do. But try as we may, we cannot just stop judging things. Judgment is what gives us choices, and free will.

So, how does one exist as a human being and not go around constantly judging everything either good or evil? How can we avoid sin, and also make   choices if the basic knowledge of good and evil is "original sin?" Deuteronomy, has the answer. The choices God has set before us are not between good or evil, blessings or curse they are between life and death, therefore "choose life."

It is a different system. It is a different way of thinking and judging.

Choose life. Such a simple directive seems to belong on a bumper sticker or a desk plaque. It has become a trendy slogan for a political group seeking neither choice nor life. It has probably filled many such purposes throughout the millennia. It can so easily be a slogan.   But its essential simplicity is deceiving.

This simple directive maps a clear road back from Hell. Every fork along the way is clearly marked, "life" or "death." So, "choose life."

A few years ago I was part of a prayer group in which we talked about people in need of special prayers then put our concern for these people into prayers. One person in our group mentioned a young teacher who had been undergoing treatment for advanced breast cancer. Her diagnosis was very bleak. She had tried chemotherapy and radiation. Then she found out about an experimental procedure for breast cancer, a bone marrow transplant. Because her cancer was taking over her body, and her chance of survival was virtually non-existent, she qualified for experimental treatments that had not been approved for use on people who would otherwise have a chance to survive.

We talked in our circle about the probable cost of such a treatment, the travel to a distant city, and the long stay in a strange town, away from her young child and her husband. We thought of our own lives, and we talked about the strain this must be putting on her family. We prayed for her, and for her family.

That treatment gave her another period of wellness, that I think was measured in months. I saw her during that time, and she was in a state of euphoria, in love with life. She savored every moment of every day, and she said, when she didn't know what to do, she simply "chose life, and it was the right thing to do."

Her cancer came back. This time, another experimental treatment was available for the otherwise "hopeless" cancer victim to try. This time, it was the stem cell transplant. Again, she took the big, complicated expensive treatment. I thought, how can she so frivolously choose life when it is so full of pain and hardship? In our group one person said out loud that he felt this woman needed simply to have the courage to face the inevitable death and not to keep putting her family through all of this expense, and false hope. I thought of what I would do if I found myself in her place. I was totally afraid of medical procedures. Death was far less frightening. It would be an easy choice for me. I promised myself that if I ever got cancer I would die the heroic no cost death, and spare my family the hardship of searching for a cure.

Now that I have tried on her shoes and taken just a few steps of her long journey, I am of a completely different

opinion. I am in that euphoric state of savoring every moment of my life. I am no more afraid of death than I ever was when I promised myself I would rather choose death. But, I can more clearly understand the choice for life.

For me, if my cancer returns, I have more life choosing options than she did. Because she did clinical trials I can qualify for a stem cell transplant without being in the final stages of cancer, when it may not be as effective. I could have a stem cell transplant, or possibly other new treatments and these might save my life, for more years. Because this woman and her family made the hard choice, for life, others, like myself have many more options, with less personal hardship.

The popular advice to give to cancer patients is "keep a positive attitude." That seems ironic, and frivolous. "You have cancer, so be positive."

But from this woman named Bonnie Shade, (Blessed Shadow,) I heard "choose life." I learned that this "positive attitude" thing is an actual possibility. A "positive attitude" is not ignorance of sorrow. It is not denial of fear and pain. It is not a blissful smile on rotting road kill. It is simply the constant walk in the direction out of Hell. To find this direction, choose life.

Celebrating 100

I saved the "7" and the "9" birthday candles from my Dad's birthday cake last year. I told Mom as we were putting the dishes away, and I wrapped those up to save, that I would be able to use them again, only reversed. I was thinking they were for Dad's cake, in the year 2015. Some people may not want to live deep into their 90's. I hear people say they hope they do not. But I know Mom and Dad were planning how they would age. Dad interviewed people who were living full lives into their older years — older than he. He wrote a newspaper column on aging. Like everything else he did, it was upbeat, and forward thinking. Now I have to let go of that plan to use those candles.

How old should I plan to become? I know I want to live to be fifty three. And I can easily see that fifty four is looking pretty good as long as I am as healthy as I am now. And what about that nifty five year survival thing, when I could be released from daily concern over a recurrence of cancer? What if I live ten more years? What if I live to be sixty, or seventy? What if I live to be one hundred?

The picture of a one hundred year old in my mind's eye is considerable better than the picture I have of an eighty year old. There are lots of eighty year olds who seem very old, and aren't the least bit happy with the life they have trudged dutifully through all these years. But, centurions, now, they are sort of beyond being elderly. Those people are bright eyed and full of wisdom. They savor life. I know that is a rash, totally unfounded generalization, but in my experience, those are the examples I can imagine.

Tom's grandfather lived until a week before his one hundredth birthday. He was bright eyed and full of wisdom for as long as he lived, even when he was eighty. He was an even ninety years older than Mariah. He rejoiced at her birth. When she was three we attended a noisy family gathering, with four generations of my husband's family present. Great Grandpa Justice took each great grandchild aside, and talked with them in a quiet room. Mariah went with him, hand in hand down to the room where the party noise was in the background. He sat down in a large chair, and had her sit on the footstool facing him. He took her tiny hands in his large old hands, and he asked her what she liked to do. He wanted to know what stories she liked, what she watched on television, if she had chances to be with other children her own age. We grown-ups would have told him all that. But he asked the three year old directly. He saw his many years as an opportunity to know lots of people, even three year olds. He actually lived his whole life.

So, when I go to creating a plan for my years to come, rather than just a hope that I could have some years to come, with no thoughts about filling them, I think, "What would I like to be doing on my one hundredth birthday?" How will I celebrate my years? What will a day be like if I get my wish for a future that is measured in decades?

To get all those years first I will probably need to bother to survive cancer, which probably will mean some intensive unscheduled visits to Hell from time to time. It means arguing doctors into believing in survival. And it means having a plan to make it worthwhile.

So here is a plan: On my hundredth birthday I would like to walk a mile, plant a tree to make the day special, to visit with someone I care about, and listen to some music. As I think in realistic terms about that day of celebration, I can see that it must be just one day of many like it. I must walk a mile everyday if I want to do that on my one hundredth birthday. Here I am forty-seven years younger than one hundred. It is time to start walking a mile every day. I will need to nurture friendships all along the way, if I expect to have a friend when I am one hundred. And I imagine I will need to know about trees, and the people who help plant them, if I want to plant a tree. Listening to music is a habit as well. All these wishes for a future have the side-effect of making each day that good. So whether or not I ever get three digits on my birthday cake, the journey will be worthwhile.

The Emptying of the Nest

Phil and Sara and their new baby Bobby, came out here from Ohio to celebrate Mariah's graduation. They were here for the baccalaureate service. Mariah played a piece on the violin that Sara had first played for her, when Mariah was her student. Jack and Liz came out for her graduation ceremony.

We climbed to the very top of the bleachers. I couldn't really get close enough to get a good picture, so why not just go to the top, and see it all, and feel the wind and rain just as it was — no hiding — no holding back. The football field was dressed up in flowers and folding chairs, all ready for the "Pomp and Circumstance" that the band had practiced earlier that day. The ribbon of all of our children unfurled into a procession, moving from the back doors of the school to the temporary chairs. Mariah was third.

A mother has to explain why. That is my job. I am a mother. My child was third because of a simple mathematical glitch. The few Advanced Placement courses that were offered were weighted. At the time the decision was made the three straight A students had taken all of the AP courses they could, but Mariah took an additional class. Some days she came to school early and took an extra German class before the school day began because she wanted to take more language than would fit into her schedule. That extra A watered down her numerical average, and so she was numerically third. There, I explained why Mariah was third. I suppose my mother had to explain that I was something like 160th in the line, because that is where "Heitzman" fell in the alphabet.

At any rate, the school recognized the glitch, and invited the three students to be the speakers, and, in fact, they barely mentioned the placement. Mariah's speech was tremendous. The out-of-town news reporter assumed she was the number one student, so they featured her picture, and quoted her speech in their article about graduations. They saw it just as I did, it was all about Mariah. We bought lots of copies of that newspaper.

As I sat there in the bleachers at dusk I remembered it was just a little over a year ago that Dr. Tallhouse said, "I see you have a sixteen year old daughter. Do you want to see her graduate from high school?" And then I pictured myself being wheeled onto the field in some medical contraption replete with dangling tubes and I.V. bottles. I imagined they would read her name, then I would gasp my last breath. I decided to aim for that dismal picture anyway. But that is not at all how it turned out. This day was better beyond my wildest imaginings. Here I was, with lots of silver hair making curls in the misty rain, a new little crepe dress, that did not in the least confine a newly found surge of energy. I danced to our perch on the top tier of bleachers. Cancer had nothing to do with this day.

From the podium, Mariah talked about our trips to New York when she was a very small child and we went to see her grandparents. I could feel those angels' eyes on us that day. She talked about crossing the George Washington Bridge. I thought of the tiny little girl in the car seat, stretching to see out of the car window, passed the girders and cables out to the wide river, bordered by the New York skyline.

Some sparrows twittered in the distant trees. I thought about wings.

When she was a very small child we lived in a small town in Ohio. One spring day like this one, I pulled her in a red wagon, down the sidewalks, to go to the grocery store. On the way we came across a fluffy grey fledgling bird all puffed up, sitting in the middle of the sidewalk. I had to pull the wagon onto the grass to pass the young bird. Mariah popped out of the wagon. I warned her not to touch it, the mother and father bird were probably watching, and would worry if she touched it. The little bird heard Mariah's little voice, and began tweeting loudly at her as if to ask for help. Mariah begged me to let her take it home, but I insisted it needed to be left alone. We went on to the store.

On the return trip, as we turned to go down that block I thought if the bird is still there, I will have to do something to protect it from cats and other children in this neighborhood. It is clearly asking for help, and food, and everything life offers. Sure enough, the bird was there. By this time, it was panting, and exhausted. It would surely die here if I didn't do something. As a child I had saved birds. Saving things is like riding a bicycle. It comes back to you when you need it. So I told Mariah we could not touch the bird with our hands. The mother and father bird would not take it back if it smelled like people. And they would know. So her job was to gather leaves and twigs to make a "nest" in the wagon. I used leaves to pick the bird up, and place it in the nest.

Once home, Mariah had the task of making a bread basket into a nest, while I heated some baby formula and egg yolk, and sterilized a medicine dropper which was to play the part of the parent bird's beak. I called the veterinarian, and he said, there was nothing we could do to save the bird. And he knew of no animal rescue group that would be interested in a now identifiable, blue jay fledgling.

The little bird's incessant squawks grew stronger almost immediately after we fed it. It's loud cries became its name, "Tweet." And when the little child had given it a name, I knew that we were committed to this creature till death parts us. Mariah had not known loss.

We put the bread basket nest high above our heads in a pine tree outside our back door. Every hour that afternoon we took it down, and gave it more food and water, and every time it heard Mariah's little voice it answered with its big loud squawky tweet.

That evening, as Mariah went to bed she wanted to hear stories of birds' lives. My silent prayer was that this little girl would find a happy ending with this little creature in our handmade nest. We looked at the picture in her favorite book of a little round headed blue bird. Tweet's first real feather was blue so it was the same, maybe. I tried to prepare Mariah for the possibility of losing Tweet. I said, "Maybe Tweet would be gone in the morning. Maybe Tweet would learn to fly with the other birds and would leave us, and go live with birds. Or maybe Tweet would learn to fly with the angels, and Tweet would leave us, but would be with God."

The next morning I opened the window near the pine tree with the bread basket nest, and no sound came from the nest. I was going outside to see, when Mariah came hurrying downstairs with this one thing on her mind. She wanted to check on Tweet. I wanted to go out there first, so I could prepare her for whatever was keeping the bird silent. As soon as Mariah spoke, the loud familiar "tweet" answered from the nest. I got the bird formula ready, and gave Mariah a project.

I told her, today we would put wild bird seed out for Tweet in case he was old enough to eat grown up bird's food. Mariah set about to prepare a little serving of seeds from our bird feeder bag. As she busied herself with this project on the back porch, I could hear lots of birds twittering in the trees outside. Tweet kept answering anything that twittered with his loud cry.

I called Mariah in for breakfast, and she explained to me in a very matter of fact way, "Tweet is gone. Tweet did not learn to fly with the angels. Before any angels came, two big blue birds came by, and when he saw them he jumped out of the basket. Then he just flew away with them. First he was in the tree, then he was gone."

What a relief that was! The only happy ending an animal story could have was this! The parents came and finished the flying lesson. The bird was safe with his blue jay family. But Mariah was disappointed, I think, that she did not see angels come for Tweet. I had, perhaps, not given God the chance to answer my prayer for a happy ending to Tweet, in the simple, natural way God so often answers. I had tried to create the happy ending myself by offering an angel option.

Before I began my journeys between Hell and Heaven, while I was living peacefully in fear of an undiagnosed breast lump, I prepared for death by writing a letter to Mariah.

"I knew all of this before I had lived it. Life is good. God is real. Death takes only part of life, not its definition. I will always love you dear child. Like a sea is full of water drops, the Holy Spirit contains a droplet of spirit that I share with you. Each time you look out on the horizon and see the sunset doubled by its own reflection you can remember that the spiritual gifts of heaven are twice a beautiful as our little earthly symbols for life."

Now, this graduation day was so full of that story of Tweet. There were all those obvious symbols, from the tiny bird growing feathers and flying to the conspicuous pun, of "the empty nest." But really, it was that happy ending that kept refreshing the story. It was the simple, but more amazing than the Red Sea parting miracle that I was experiencing at that moment. Simply, life is good.

AFTERWORDS

This is a listing of updates to tie up loose ends.

In August, 1998, the families of Munro's and Heitzman's gathered in a small town in Illinois for a "Celebration of the Love and Lives of Rosie and Milt Heitzman." The participation of various family members enriched this worship event. My cousin Carol is a pastor, and she led the service. Aunt Ginnie played the violin. That of course, was a testimony to the power of healing. But the piece she played was the violin part of a trio written by her daughter, Sandra Hearne. The other parts of the trio were Sandra, playing the piano, and my mother's and Ginnie's brother singing the tenor solo. The words were poems my mother had written.

Mariah also played the violin in that service. She played a movement of Vivaldi's *Spring Concerto*." And she read my father's prayer for the "The Blessing of the Fleet" as the benediction.

Mom had reproduced many prints of one of her pen and ink sketches that accompanied a poem she had written. Each time my father performed a wedding she presented the bride and groom with this sailboat print, and poem. She was evidently planning on enough future weddings that we had an adequate supply of these to provide each person at the memorial service with a print. The picture and the poem are included in the front of this book.

***

That memorial service was in August, then in September I heard reports that the FDA had approved two new cancer treatments. One was the stem cell transplant for breast cancer, and the other was the use of Hercepton. Once upon a time my plan was simply to survive until these things were available with insurance. And now I have. But, now I am sort of imagining my life continuing without any need for further treatment. That is probably like buying a lottery ticket the morning after you win a sweepstakes. How many happy endings does one story need?

***

The investigator that we hired to find the cause of the car crash went to New York and met Jack there. They found that the car was no longer impounded at the police lot. It had evidentially been released by the insurance company without our signature, and against our wishes. But Jack located it at a junk yard, and the investigator went with him, and pointed out the component that Jack was to remove and purchase. (Due to a law in New York we could not buy the whole car back.) The part the investigator wanted was the air bag in the steering wheel. We were a bit surprised that he could do his research without taking any sensors or any other part, but that is what he felt was needed. Jack retrieved that and forwarded it to his office in New Mexico.

***

In 1998 some GM cars were recalled for having air bags that deployed without an accident. Saturn was not among these, even though the components which make up the Saturn air bag systems are common among various GM cars. This recall, according to the news items I could find, was in response to living customer's complaints. It was not because of deaths. Dead people don't complain.

***

The lawsuit against me was settled.

***

In September of 1998, we found ourselves crossing the George Washington Bridge more often, since Mariah is in New York, at a small College in Bronxville. Reading her e-mail is like hearing from a thirsty traveler, stopping at a dessert oasis. She is drinking in the wonders the world offers a bright young mind, like a thirsty traveler enjoys a cool drink of water.

***

In October, 1998 I learned that doctors are no longer recommending the stem cell transplant for breast cancer because it does not seem to offer any benefit over standard chemo therapy. So my decision based on economy was perhaps the best after all.

***

In March, 1999, I was again in Dr. Finn's office, for my annual checkup, and I was amazed to see that he had installed a juke box in his waiting room! There it was next to the fish tank, flashing neon, with a rack of 45 r.p.m. records just waiting for our quarters. I flipped through the menu of old songs. I could tell by the glances from the other silver haired patients that a well spent quarter in this juke box probably would not be playing "Great Balls of Fire." So I sat down quietly and read the only magazine left on the rack, "Sports Illustrated."

***

Our investigation of the car crash stalled in the hands of the professional we hired. After we heard nothing for a year, and had paid him considerably more than the original estimate, I gave up on his expertise. I wrote and asked him to wrap up his investigation. Then I just gathered up all the information I could find, and drew up the most logical conclusions that I could come up with. I added Jack's analysis and photos, and a set of aerial photos, along with the various reports: police reports, autopsies, E.R. report, etc. I put it all together in a box. Then I wrote a letter very simply stating that Jack and I believe that the air bag killed our mother, and caused the crash that killed our father, as well. I sent this single paragraph conclusion to Saturn, General Motors, the National Highway Safety Transportation Administration, and the National Safety Council.

Thirty hours after I mailed it, a woman from Saturn Product Improvement Division called. Jack and I were totally surprised and elated. We had no idea they would care to hear what we had to say. But they did. I sent her my report and Jack's report and photos. Later she told us the information was posted on the company computer system. To me, that was like having that empty chair at the conference table. She forwarded our information to their investigators. I have sent them the various reports and photos we have collected. We continue to be in dialogue with them.

Their investigators went to the wrecked car and retrieved the real air bag module, we then knew for sure that the investigator was no expert on air bags. He evidently did not even know where to find the air bag module on the Saturn.

***

A few weeks after I sent the letter, The National Safety Council sent us their condolences.

***

Three months after I sent the letter, The National Highway Safety Transportation Administration sent me a letter offering condolences, and explaining that such things cannot be investigated, but it said that "customer complaints" are recorded. I think they may be avoiding the problem of dead people that way. They also gave a telephone number of their investigative unit. And, yes, I am confused by this answer. But the letter was clearly consistent with the telephone conversation I had with them two years ago.

***

Even after two Christmas's without parents, I still catch myself wondering what to give them for their gift this year. They need so little. But I wish I could give them more.

***

Now it is the year 2000, and I still say, "life is good." This evening we are sitting in the living room. I had a chance to work for the lawn furniture designer again last Fall. I bought a coffee table from them that is metal, the satin silver color of stainless steel. Paradoxically it is an organic form, like a mushroom stem with a glass top. It gives me a sense of peace, new growth and fearlessness. It makes the living room seem right.

Tom is looking over these words which I have put on paper. We are talking about what to do with this journal. Perhaps I will share it with you in a book.

***

Milton's Prayer for the Blessing of the Fleet
Orient, New York, 1997

Our Father, Creator of the Universe, Maker of the seas and Calmer of the winds at sea, we offer our thanks for the love and protective care you give to all of us.

We thank You for the calm beauty and the turbulent tempests of the sea itself.

We thank you for the crafts that carry us for fun and commerce. Yes, Lord, we thank you for this moment and ask your blessing upon each of us and our families.

We ask that you will truly bless each vessel and give wisdom and good fortune to the one who guides that craft. May they continue to have safe journeys and enjoy an expanded appreciation of the world you have given them today.

O God, our Heavenly Father we thank you for this moment and the days to come. Bless us all. AMEN

ABOUT THE AUTHOR...

Julie Marlin is a graphics artist for a newspaper by day. Her husband pastors a United Church of Christ, in East Greenville, Pennsylvania. The family collie has claimed the room of Mariah, her daughter, who is usually away at Sarah Lawrence College, in Bronxville, New York.

For many years Julie has been writing biblically based plays and musicals, including musicals, *Ruth the Love Story*, and *Olive's Twigs and Pits Traveling Medicine Show*. Soon to be released is, *Wilderness Options* a series of dramatic vignettes, based on the gospel of Matthew and including a full length liturgical, passion play.

Julie received a Bachelor of Arts degree from Eureka College, in Eureka, Illinois, and Master's of Arts, with emphasis on Christian Drama from Methodist Theological School in Delaware, Ohio.

ORDER FORM

NAME_____

Address_____

City_____State_____Zip_____

Phone_(_____)_____

Please send me _____ copies of
LIVING ROOM: A Visitor's Guide to Hell & Heaven
 by Julie Marlin   ISBN 0-9700813-7-5

Number of copies _____
  x $14.95 (ea.) = Total for books _____
              Plus shipping + $3.20
    (PA. Resident, only add 6.% sales tax)_____
          TOTAL AMOUNT $_____

☐Enclosed is my check for $_____

☐Please bill me when my books are
  shipped.

Please send me information about future
books, plays and stories from Wild Grace.
   ☐ Inspirational Books
   ☐ Church Plays and Musicals

FAX: 215-679-6684 or send to:
         WILD GRACE
         P.O. Box 194
         Red Hill, PA 18076